The **Savvy Backpacker's Guide** to

Europe
ON A BUDGET

D0834412

The **Savvy Backpacker's Guide** to

Europe
ON A BUDGET

Advice on Trip Planning, Packing, Hostels & Lodging,
Transportation & More!

James Feess

Skyhorse Publishing

Skyhorse Publishing books may be purchased in bulk at special discounts for sales promotion, corporate gifts, fund-raising, or educational purposes. Special editions can also be created to specifications. For details, contact the Special Sales Department, Skyhorse Publishing, 307 West 36th Street, 11th Floor, New York, NY 10018 or info@skyhorsepublishing.com.

Skyhorse® and Skyhorse Publishing® are registered trademarks of Skyhorse Publishing, Inc.®, a Delaware corporation.

Visit our website at www.skyhorsepublishing.com.

10 9 8 7 6 5 4 3 2

Library of Congress Cataloging-in-Publication Data is available on file.

Cover design by Liz Driesbach
Cover photo credit Thinkstock

Print ISBN: 978-1-62914-738-3
Ebook ISBN: 978-1-63220-114-0

Printed in China

Table of Contents

CHAPTER SIX—SOLO AND GROUP TRAVEL................. 133

CHAPTER FIVE—TRAVEL SAFETY AND AVOIDING TOURIST SCAMS 119

CHAPTER SEVEN—DAY-TO-DAY MONEY SAVING STRATEGIES 143

Introduction

For many people, the thought of traveling to Europe is intimidating, or at the very least, confusing. It's perfectly normal to feel a little overwhelmed by the whole planning process. I know felt the exact same way when I was preparing for my first backpacking trip through Europe. I'd never before used public transportation, I spoke only English, I had no concept of hostels, and this trip would be the first time I was truly self-reliant. It did feel daunting at times, but it was also exciting because I knew I was about to have the experience of a lifetime.

Every year, Europe enchants millions of visitors with her countless charms while she happily drains their bank accounts. However, savvy travelers know it doesn't require a lot of money to have an incredible journey abroad. In fact, the more money you spend the larger wedge you'll drive between you and the local culture. When you travel on a tight budget, you'll have a more authentic experience because you'll find yourself perusing the same neighborhood markets, shopping at the same grocery stores, and eating at the same restaurants as the locals.

Luckily, Europe has plenty of inexpensive places to sleep, the public transportation is amazing, and food can be affordable. The infrastructure for budget travel is already in place—you simply need to learn the travel skills to take full advantage of it. However, if you're not aware of these budget-travel strategies your bank account will take a beating.

It's important to realize that budget travel is more than just saving money. It's also about knowing how to spend your money wisely in order to maximize your travel time—which is just as valuable. All it takes to plan a successful journey is preparation, strategic budgeting tips, and time-tested travel advice.

I think proper travel planning is essential if you want to get the most bang for your travel buck. That said, people often tell me that they don't want to plan anything and they prefer to "play everything by ear." I understand. I was one of those people on my first trip to Europe. I had romantic notions of showing up in a city on a whim, finding a hostel, and then discovering an amazing little café frequented by locals. In reality, I spent hours trying to find a hostel only to discover that all the cheap rooms were booked. Then I couldn't locate any affordable restaurants, so I finally gave in and ate at McDonald's. That's when I realized the importance of planning

However, I want to strongly emphasize that over-planning is also a surefire path to failure and any experienced traveler will tell you the critical importance of spontaneity and flexibility. You need to plan just enough to give your trip structure and then fill the rest in as you go.

The goal of this book is to equip you with the travel knowledge needed to plan an amazing journey through Europe. Then once you're fully informed about all of your options, you can make an educated choice of which tips and advice best suits your travel style.

CHAPTER ONE— PLANNING

The secret to traveling cheaply and sucessfully all starts with a bit of planning. First there are basic matters like getting a passport and sorting out your banking, but the real planning starts when you assemble your itinerary and set your travel budget. It will take a decent amount of effort, but you'll be rewarded once you're abroad.

Big Picture Itinerary Planning

Europe is an amazingly diverse continent and it offers something for everyone. In fact, most visitors have a terribly difficult time narrowing down exactly what they want to experience because there is so much to choose from. You could travel for a year and still feel like you've missed something. Unfortunately, most of us don't have the luxury of being able to spend months traveling, so we have to economize our time.

I'll tell you right now that trying to assemble an itinerary will cause a great deal of frustration and stress. But that's okay; it is all part of the process. It takes a lot of creativity, I and you'll spend multiple hours nailing down your itinerary. In this section, I'll give you my planning strategies, but my way isn't the only method. Use these tips as a guideline, but ultimately it is up to you to find the one that works the best for your journey.

You may find it useful to go through the entire book and then return to this chapter because you'll have a better idea about transportation, travel costs, and other important travel issues so you can create a better-informed itinerary.

STEP ONE—Estimate your travel budget. For most people, money is the main limiting factor when it comes to travel planning, so it's wise to look at your finances to figure out how much you can spend on your trip. It's fine if you only have a ballpark figure, but it is very helpful to have a dollar amount that you don't want to cross. As you proceed through the next steps, you'll need to keep this amount in mind because it will be a major factor in dictating how and where you travel.

STEP TWO—Pick your approximate travel dates. Now that you have an idea of your budget, it's time to choose when and how long you want to travel. Some people travel as long as they can or until the money runs out—which is a perfectly fine way to travel; however, most travelers don't have this luxury since school, work, or other obligations usually determine when they can go abroad.

During these beginning stages, it's not necessary to know your exact travel dates, although, you should have a fairly good idea. You'll inevitably fine-tune and tweak your itinerary as you continue to plan—maybe you'll see that you can actually travel longer than you anticipated or maybe you'll realize the need to cut back. Keep in mind that flexibility is vital if you want to save money; sometimes moving your departure or return date by a day or two can save hundreds of dollars.

Want to see the Tour de France end in Paris? Mark it down on your calendar and plan around it.

STEP THREE—Write down anything you are 100% certain you are going to do. Sometimes you have things on your trip that can't change—maybe you have concert tickets or your rich uncle is letting you shack up in his fancy Tuscan villa for a week. You'll have to plan around these events so they'll greatly affect your other travel plans.

STEP FOUR—Break out the map and start brainstorming where you want to visit. I'd start off by surveying a map to become more familiar with the geography of Europe. This is helpful because you can see where all the major cities are located in relation to each other, and you'll get a better idea of the distance between areas.

Next, go to the bookstore and spend a few hours thumbing through the travel books. Take out the good ol' pen and paper. Jot down anything that looks interesting. Naturally, a lot of people will first head to the Internet for advice, but I prefer to stick with guidebooks at this stage. Guidebooks are nice because the information is organized logically and easy to find. Don't get me wrong, I love the Internet and we'll use it quite often during the following stages of the planning process, but at this point I find old-fashioned guidebooks to be the most efficient.

Don't limit yourself at this point; just brainstorm and compile a list. You'll probably end up discovering a lot of really cool places that you may have never considered.

Don't forget to keep in mind the type of stuff you're interested in experiencing—museums, party destinations, castles, beaches, major cities, small towns, cuisine, nature, music festivals, outdoor sports, etc.

Then create a map using Google Maps and place a pin in every location on your list. This is a great way to visualize everything, and maybe you'll start to see your interests guiding you to certain regions.

STEP FIVE—Start to narrow down your list. This is where things get a little more difficult. I suggest separating all the places on your list into three categories; 1) places you 100% want to see, 2) places you really want to see, and 3) places you could live without.

STEP SIX—Write down how many days you think you will want to spend in each location. Most guidebooks will give you an idea of how much time you should spend in each location (e.g. four days in Paris, three days in Berlin, four days in London, etc.). If you're like most people, you'll quickly realize there is no way you can see all the places on your list. Time to make more cuts and adjustments.

Naturally, you want to see as much as possible when you travel, but this often leads to packing way too much into the itinerary. Nearly everyone does it, and I'm guilty of it myself. I *highly suggest* resisting the temptation of attempting to see everything. I cringe every time I see someone wanting to visit London, Paris, Amsterdam, Rome, Berlin, and Barcelona in twelve days. It's possible but you'll barely scratch the surface of the places you visit.

Additionally, traveling at breakneck speeds is not only exhausting, but it will also cause major burnout. You won't give yourself the time to appreciate what you're seeing, and after a few weeks you will hardly remember what you've seen. Trust me. Ask anyone who has done a whirlwind tour and they will all tell you that they wish they had slowed down.

Don't forget to take travel time into consideration. It is easy to forget that traveling from place to place takes a lot of time, and "whirlwind" travelers should pay special attention to this. In addition to the plane or train ride, there are a lot of little additional activities that eat into your precious travel time. For example, it takes time to pack your bags, check out of your hostel, travel to the train station, and wait for your train (you'll also need to arrive a little early so as not to miss your train). Once you arrive to the new city, you have to find the hostel (hopefully you don't get lost), check in, and get settled in. All of this extra time can easily take a few hours and quickly adds up if you change locations every few days.

STEP SEVEN—Rework itinerary. Now that you have a better idea of how long to spend in each location, you can start to choose your top destinations and eliminate destinations that will not realistically fit into your schedule.

STEP EIGHT—Plot your route. Create a Google Map with each location on your list and see if there is a logical route to take. Be sure the route you take makes logical sense— e.g., don't backtrack as it wastes valuable travel time. If you have one location that is considerably farther away from all the others, you might consider skipping it, because it may not be worth the time and expense for going out of your way.

STEP NINE—Explore arrival and departure airports. The airports which you arrive into and depart from will not only affect the amount you'll pay for the ticket, but it will also shape your travel route. The largest (and usually most affordable) airports are in London, Amsterdam, Paris, Frankfurt, and Madrid—although you might find good deals at other locations so search around.

It's important to note that you don't have to arrive and depart from the same airport (this is called an open-jaw ticket). In fact, it often makes more sense to use different airports because it means you're not forced to travel in a circuit. For example, if you arrive in London but spend the next few weeks traveling south into Spain, it would be a waste of time and money to travel all the way back to London just to catch a flight. In this case, flying back home via Madrid is a smarter choice.

STEP TEN—Estimate transportation costs and travel time. Once you have a good idea of where you want to travel, you'll need to figure out transportation options and costs between each location. You basically have four choices—plane, train (rail pass or single tickets), car, or coach. Each has its own advantages and disadvantages. Read the transportation chapter to get a better idea of travel costs and options. For a quick reference about travel times and costs, visit rome2rio.com—it isn't perfect and the prices aren't always accurate but it will give a rough cost estimate.

Don't forget that your time is just as valuable as money—especially if you are on a tight timeframe. For example, the $50 coach journey from Paris to Marseilles may be $80 cheaper than taking the train, but the journey will take thirteen hours—compared to a little over three hours for the train. I know I'd rather pay the extra money to save a full day of travel.

Night trains are a decent way to travel long distances without missing a travel day. This also eliminates the need to pay for a hostel bed. It might not be very comfortable, but you can sleep in a normal seat. For an extra fee, you can get a bed in a sleeper car—although you'll be sharing a room with a few strangers. Either way, don't expect to sleep like a baby.

STEP ELEVEN—Reevaluate your route with transportation costs included. Now that you have a better idea of the costs of transportation, look back at your budget and make sure you're still on track. If transportation expenses are eating too much into your budget, you may consider altering the itinerary (or cutting back elsewhere).

Consider staying in fewer locations for a longer amount of time if your transportation costs are too high. Not only does this allow you to get to know each location better, it also gives you a chance to take day-trips to nearby areas. For example, the Château de Versailles, Château de Fontainebleau, Giverny, and

Reims are less than an hour's train ride from Paris.

STEP TWELVE—Tweak and finalize. Go back through your itinerary until you've decided on a fairly finalized travel plan. I find it helpful to write out the finalized itinerary on a calendar because it's a good way to visualize the entire journey.

STEP THIRTEEN—Realize your itinerary is flexible. One of the beautiful things about traveling through Europe is the freedom to change your plans as you wish. During my first trip, I wanted to see only big cities, but after about two weeks I needed a change of pace—so I hopped a train to a small Swiss mountain town for a few days.

The purpose of putting some thought into your itinerary isn't to lock yourself into a rigid schedule. The goal is to give your travel plans some structure and for you to be aware of all the possible travel options. It should help you best utilize your precious time abroad so you don't make any expensive travel mistakes.

Additional Itinerary Planning Advice

Start in an easy country. Traveling to a foreign country can be intimidating—especially if you don't speak the local language. If you're a little apprehensive, consider starting in an English-speaking destination. London is a great place to fly into. Not only is London a world-class city, but it is also one of the cheapest places to fly into, and it has vast connections to the rest of Europe.

Eastern Europe and Southern Europe are cheaper. If you're on a tight budget, consider spending less time in pricy Western Europe and more in Eastern and Southern Europe. Popular Eastern cities like Prague, Berlin, Krakow, and Budapest are still a bargain when compared to their Western counterparts—but their prices are slowly creeping up as more travelers discover their charms.

Stop and smell the roses. Transportation eats a huge chunk of your travel budget and is time consuming. Cut those travel costs by spending more time in fewer destinations. Additionally, you can focus on visiting a single country or on a specific geographical region. This gives you the opportunity to better explore the local culture and discover the small things you'd probably miss at first glance.

Relaxation time. Most travelers focus on hopping between Europe's major cities. There is nothing wrong with this travel style, but scheduling a few relaxing destinations will be a welcome reprieve from the constant noise and chaos of the city. It will give your mind and body some much needed opportunities to decompress.

Short trips require better time management. Generally, shorter trips require more planning than longer trips because your time is more valuable. If you only have two or three weeks, consider spending more time planning and try to minimize the time you spend traveling. If you're traveling for a few months then you can cut back on the pre-planning.

Save money, but lose some flexibility, by booking in advance. You can save a significant amount of money if you book flights and some train tickets in advance (read the transportation chapters for more details). Cheaper hostel beds are the first to be booked in the summer so you might be left with only the more expensive options if you don't book a little early.

However, booking in advance does require quite a bit more planning and you'll lose flexibility because advance cheap tickets are usually nonrefundable. It's up to you to decide which is more important.

Overestimate travel costs. Leave a little padding in your budget for unexpected expenses. Many budget travelers plan their trips around spending the bare minimum but run out of money before the end of the trip. Overestimating your travel costs will help create an emergency fund to get you out of those sticky situations.

Become familiar with transportation. High-speed trains, long-distance trains, local trains, regional trains, suburban trains, trams, subways, city buses, coaches, ferries . . . For many travelers, this is the first time using such a complex and vast transportation network so it can seem a little overwhelming. Take a little time to read up on how everything works. It isn't too complicated, but everything will go a lot smoother if you do a little homework beforehand.

Estimating Daily Travel Costs

The main daily costs associated with travel include accommodation, food, sightseeing, public transportation, and a few extra incidental costs. Most frugal-minded, hostel-hopping backpackers spend around $70–$100/day in Western Europe and $40–$70/day in Eastern Europe. At this level, you can travel fairly modestly and comfortably without making too many sacrifices. If you watch your budget closely and make a conscious effort to keep your costs down, it's possible to drop your expenses by around 25%–30%. Lowering your costs even more starts to become difficult so you'll have to get creative—there are plenty of money-saving tips throughout this book.

It is also important to note that these daily costs do not include long-distance transportation between destinations—this is just for estimating how much you'll spend on an average day.

ACCOMMODATION COST ESTIMATE

For this example I am going to assume that you'll be staying in hostels since that is the most popular form of accommodation for budget travelers. However, there are other options, so check out the accommodation chapter for more information about short-term apartments, couchsurfing, camping, and a few others.

Hostel prices can vary greatly from city to city. Many raise their rates on the weekend (Friday–Saturday) and some holidays.

The rates on the next page are based on a late June booking from hostels that received fairly high reviews from past guests. You may be able to find cheaper options if you're willing to overlook cleanliness, a good location, or other desirable amenities.

Furthermore, the prices listed are for a single person in the cheapest room available (usually in a room with anywhere from 6 to 20 beds). The prices generally get more expensive as the number of beds in a room decreases (e.g., an 18-bed room will be cheaper than a 4-bed room). The price also goes up Friday and Saturday. Private rooms (for two people) are normally two or three times as expensive as the cheapest bed.

London: $20–$45
Paris: $30–$50
Dublin: $15–$25
Amsterdam: $20–$50
Munich: $20–$40
Berlin: $13–$30
Krakow: $7–$18
Budapest: $8–$20
Barcelona: $15–$25

FOOD COST ESTIMATE

Europe is home to some of the world's greatest cuisine and as a budget backpacker you'll have little money to try it. (Sorry.) Simply put, frequently eating at restaurants is a temptingly easy way to blow your budget. Nonetheless, I do encourage that everyone set aside some cash for trying the local cuisine, given that food is such a large part of experiencing a country's culture—it would be a shame to miss this experience.

For the budget traveler, the daily food budget will be anywhere from $14 to $40. At the lower end of this price range, you'll mostly be eating the free hostel breakfast and homemade meals/picnics from the grocery store. At the middle range you can eat at cheap takeaway restaurants ($8–$10 for a meal), affordable sit-down restaurants ($15–$20 for a meal), and maybe have a few snacks throughout the day.

I suggest budgeting a little high for food because even the most diehard budget travelers will break down and buy a prepared meal sometimes. You will too, trust me. When you're not familiar with the city it can be challenging to find a grocery store and it's even worse when you're already really hungry.

Additionally, making a meal after a long day of sightseeing can sometimes be a pain in the ass, so it will often be challenging to motivate yourself to cook something.

SIGHTSEEING AND ATTRACTIONS COST ESTIMATE

You go to Europe to experience the culture and to see the sights. Well, get out your wallet because most attractions charge an admission fee. The fees are usually not outrageous but they do add up. Many places offer student/youth discounts so be sure to inquire about those. While you may not do something that requires an admission fee every day, I would still budget about $15/day for sightseeing. Here is a list of admissions prices at some popular attractions in Europe so you can get a feel of how much things cost:

Louvre Museum – Paris: $17
Centre Pompidou Museum – Paris: $18
Tower of London: $37
Van Gogh Museum – Amsterdam: $20
Walking Tours: Free (guides work on tips) or $15 for paid tours
Note: Many museums offer discounted or free tickets to students and/or people under the age of twenty-six.

PUBLIC TRANSPORTATION COST ESTIMATE

Between subways, buses, and trams, European public transportation is excellent in nearly every large and medium-sized city. Additionally, it's usually affordable. Most cities are walkable and I always suggest walking when possible, but in some cases public transport might be a better use of your time and energy.

Most cities sell a range of tickets and travel passes (e.g., single tickets, 1, 3, 5, 7 day passes, month pass, etc.) so it's smart to do a little research to find the option that works best for you. Below are some examples of transportation cost:
London Tube (w/Oyster Card): $4/off-peak single fare or $14/all day
Paris Metro: $19 for 10 one-way tickets
Amsterdam (tram): $23 for 72 hours of unlimited travel
Budapest (bus and subway): $17 for 72 hours of unlimited travel about
Prague: $1.60 for a single tram ticket
Barcelona (metro): $1.40 for a single ticket on the metro

ALCOHOL COST ESTIMATE

Europe has an insane amount of good beer and wine, so it would be a shame to not sample a few gallons. And, let's be honest, most backpackers drink their fair share as they travel around. Just be cautious because those big nights out can cost you a fortune—but I don't have to tell you that. As always, buying alcohol from the grocery store is a great way to save a lot of money.

Listed below are some sample alcohol prices from around Europe:

London (Pint of Beer): $3.10–$6.20 but expect to pay more at trendy clubs/pubs.

Paris (Wine): $7–$12 cheap bottle of good wine from the store.

Prague (Pint of Beer): Restaurant $1.90 and around $.70 from a grocery store.

Budapest (Pint of Beer): $2–$3 at a bar

Munich (Beer): $9 for a huge mug at a beer garden and around $1 for a liter of beer from the store.

EXTRAS AND UNEXPECTED EXPENSES ESTIMATE

Don't forget to add a little extra money into your budget for unexpected expenses like laundry, souvenirs, toiletries, clothing, skydiving, missed trains, etc. On my first trip abroad, I barely missed one of my flights because the train to the airport was delayed. I had to pay an extra $100 to change flights. Of course, I hadn't left much room in my budget for unexpected expenses, so I had to cut back on other areas.

Money Matters

Having a solid grasp on exchange rates, currencies, ATM fees, credit card fees, and other banking issues won't only save you quite a bit of money, but it will also save you a lot of hassle.

UNDERSTANDING CURRENCY AND EXCHANGE RATES

The **Euro** was first introduced in 1999 as a way to provide common currency across Europe. Currently, this single currency is shared by a large number of European countries. This is helpful for visitors because you no longer have to exchange money each time you visit a new country.

Here is a list of the countries that use the Euro: Andorra, Austria, Belgium, Cyprus, Estonia, Finland, France, Germany, Greece, Ireland, Italy, Kosovo, Latvia, Luxembourg, Malta, Monaco, Montenegro, Netherlands, Portugal, San Marino, Slovakia, Slovenia, Spain, and Vatican City.

However, there are still some countries that haven't adopted the Euro and still use their own currency. These countries are: Albania, Belarus, Bosnia, Bulgaria, Croatia, Czech Republic, Denmark, Herzegovina, Hungary, Iceland, Liechtenstein, Lithuania, FYR Macedonia, Moldova, Norway, Poland, Romania, Russia, Serbia, Slovakia, Sweden, Switzerland, Ukraine, and the United Kingdom (England, Northern Ireland, Scotland, and Wales).

The **Exchange Rate** is the value of one currency in terms of another. The rates change daily (although in tiny increments). Be sure to know the current exchange rate while you're traveling so you'll have a better idea what you're spending in your home currency. I like to write down in my notebook how much currencies are worth compared to the US dollar so I can have a quick reference when I make purchases. I use XE.com to find the current rates—they also have an excellent free exchange rate app that can be used without an Internet connection if you travel with a smartphone.

It is fairly simple to estimate prices on the fly with the Euro, British Pound Sterling, and the Swiss Franc because those currencies are relatively similar to the US dollar. For example, 10 USD = 7.31 EUR, 6.12 GBP, and 9 CHF. However, it gets more

11

confusing in other countries because the numbers get significantly higher so it is more difficult to estimate how much you're paying for things. For example, 10 USD is worth about 2,185 Hungarian Forint. Now, before you get too excited, this doesn't mean you can live like a king on $10. It just means that a meal and a beer at an inexpensive restaurant in Budapest will cost about 2,185 HUF.

WITHDRAWING MONEY FROM AN ATM

The ATM is easily the best way to get cash while traveling in Europe. There are ATMs everywhere (airports, train stations, scattered across cities, etc.) and it's the most popular (and sometimes only) way for Europeans to access their cash. Most ATMs have an English language option (look for the little British flag icon), so you don't have to worry about knowing the local language. Another benefit is that you will be given the current exchange rate when you make a withdrawal (money change offices give you a poor conversion rate).

Only use a debit card at the ATM. If you use a credit card, the transaction is considered a cash advance so

you'll be hit with huge fees and high interest rates. Additionally, make sure your debit card is attached to your main checking account because you won't be able to withdraw from a secondary checking account or a savings account.

Your debit card must have a four-digit PIN code. Some cards use a six-digit code but those won't work in European cash machines.

Check compatibility. Ensure your debit card has either a Cirrus or Plus logo on them (any Visa or MasterCard will have one). Cards with these logos are the most widely accepted throughout Europe. American Express and Discover are accepted in some locations but not nearly as much as Visa or MasterCard.

Contact your bank about their fees. One great thing about ATMs in Europe is that they don't charge you a fee when you use them—even if it's not your bank. However, your home bank will probably charge you a flat fee (usually between $1 and $5) and/or an "international transaction fee" that is usually 1–3% of the amount withdrawn. Pay attention to these charges because they can add up quickly—especially if your bank charges $5 each time you make a withdrawal. Obviously, if your bank charges a high flat fee it is wiser to withdraw large chunks of cash to reduce the amount of fees charged.

Banks are always switching up their fees so you'll have to do a little research to find the best option. NerdWallet.com is a good source for updated information about which cards are the best for international travel.

Have a backup card in case something happens to your card. Every time I put my card into a foreign ATM, I have the sinking feeling the machine will eat it—that's why I prefer to use them only during business hours. Once, while traveling in France, I entered my PIN incorrectly three times (I was using the wrong card) and the machine took the card. I talked to the banker inside and they said it couldn't be retrieved. Luckily I had another card; without it, I would not have had a way to get money. If your card does get stuck, and there isn't a message on screen telling you why it's not being returned, cancel your card—this is one method thieves use to tamper with ATMs to steal people's cards.

Check your daily withdrawal limits. Some banks put a daily limit on how much cash you can withdraw. Additionally, the ATM may also limit how much you can withdraw. If you're on a budget you probably won't reach the limit but it is good to keep in mind.

Pay attention to your surroundings. Be aware when you're using the ATM because it's one area that thieves and scammers love to target. First, if anything about the machine looks strange, find another one. It isn't uncommon for thieves to install cameras and fake keypads on ATMs in an effort to steal your information. Always cover the keypad with your hand as you enter your PIN.

Keep an eye on your surroundings as you use the machine. Once, as my wife was using an ATM in Paris, three young children approached her. One of them pulled on her arm and another reached around and pushed the button for €300. Luckily, she was able to grab all the cash before the kids got any of it. This scam is very popular throughout Europe. If you find yourself in this situation focus on the money and not the kids because they want you to turn your back to the ATM.

Don't use a debit card to make purchases. Only use your ATM card to access cash from the ATM—for everything else use a credit card. This is because it is very easy to copy (aka clone) a bankcard. All the thief (usually a waiter or a shopkeeper) needs to do is swipe your card with a special card reader that instantly copies all the information off the magnetic strip. The info can then be transferred onto a blank card or saved on a computer to be used later. They can then rack up tons of charges without you even knowing.

You want to avoid using your debit card to make purchases because it's tied directly to your checking account so the money is gone as soon as the card is used. A thief can easily drain your account (usually collecting tons of overdraft fees in the process) and it is much harder to reverse the charges. Most banks offer theft protection but it can take weeks to get your money back. Additionally, your card will be canceled so you won't be able to use ATMs anymore—which means you won't have access to cash.

However, if your credit card is cloned, you don't have to worry because the card isn't tied to your bank account. You'll just have to cancel the card and your credit card company will stop the unauthorized charges. You might have to fill out some paperwork but that's about it.

USING CREDIT CARDS IN EUROPE

Credit cards are accepted throughout Europe; however, many smaller shops may have a minimum purchase amount or may not accept cards so always have cash. Visa and MasterCard are the most widely accepted cards. Some places might accept American Express or Discover, but I wouldn't count on it.

Research the fees. Most credit card companies charge a 1%–3% fee each time the card is used internationally, but there are a few cards that waive all foreign transaction fees. NerdWallet.com keeps an updated list of cards and how much they charge. Do be sure to read the fine print about annual fees and all of that fun stuff.

Have a backup card. It's a good idea to bring a few credit cards while traveling just in case one gets lost or stolen. Obviously, don't keep all your cards in the same place.

American cards don't work everywhere. Over the past few years, Europe has converted to chip-and-pin debit and credit cards—while American cards use magnetic stripes. In a nutshell, the chip-and-pin cards have an embedded microchip and, instead of signing a receipt, the user enters a PIN code to authorize the transaction (obviously using a PIN code to authorize

a transaction is much more secure than a signature). At the moment, most merchants still accept magnetic stripe cards but some may refuse or be confused how to swipe the card—especially in smaller towns.

The main problem arises at self-service machines—like train station and subway ticket machines, self-serve gas stations, toll roads, and bike rental stations. These machines will often only accept the chip-and-pin cards; so again, it is a good idea to always have cash.

Some US banks are starting to offer chip-and-pin cards to their customers but it's still fairly rare.

Pay in local currency. Sometimes the merchant will ask if you'd like to be charged in your home currency—it's called a Dynamic Currency Conversion (DCC). This may sound like a good idea but it's really just a way to scam you out of a little more money. Basically, when the company does the conversion, they use an unfavorable exchange rate and you pay more. Plus, sometimes your home bank still converts the charge and does its own exchange rate—so you're essentially penalized twice. If you see anything on the receipt other than the local currency, there is a good chance they used DCC.

Everyone loves cash. I know I've mentioned this a few times before, but it's important: always have cash. You'll run into a lot of situations when you'll need it. Many small restaurants, green grocers, and street food vendors will only accept cash.

ALTERNATIVE WAYS TO ACCESS MONEY

Prepaid debit cards. Over the past few years, the usage of prepaid cards has exploded. Using a prepaid card while traveling can have its advantages but they rarely outweigh the disadvantages. These cards are used like credit cards so you don't put your bank account at risk if the card is stolen. Additionally, many, but not all, cards offer theft protection so they're a bit safer than cash. Some cards can be reloaded with funds, making it a simple way for people back home to send you money.

However, prepaid cards come with a lot of extra fees so read all the fine print. There is usually an "activation fee" and a fee for adding money to the balance. Many charge a monthly maintenance fee and inactivity fees. Additionally, there will be a fee each time you use the ATM and prepaid cards can often have a worse exchange rate than normal debit cards. All the extra fees can quickly outweigh all positive aspects of a prepaid card, so do your homework.

Travelers cheques. Travelers cheques fell out of fashion about twenty years ago, so not many people really use them anymore. It can be dif-

ficult to find a place that accepts them, so they aren't worth the trouble. They are fine as an emergency fund, but quite impractical for frequent use.

Money exchange offices. I like to bring a hundred-dollar bill in case of an emergency, but other than that I don't recommend bringing any cash from home. You'll need to exchange your cash for the local currency, and you'll get hit with commissions and poor exchange rates. The only time I'd use an exchange office is if I have a lot of extra local currency at the end of my trip and I want US dollars, or if I'm visiting another country that doesn't use the Euro.

You'll find money exchange offices in any major airport, train station, and scattered throughout cities. The offices in airports and train stations give the worst exchange rates so it's better to use the exchange offices in the city (do avoid tourist areas). Always count the money before you leave the exchange office—even legitimate exchange offices might "forget" to give you the correct amount.

And please, never change your money on the street. A "helpful" local that offers to do it for you is always a scam. They'll use sleight of hand and confusion to replace large bills with small denomination bills or they'll just give you a terrible exchange rate.

Travel Documents

Get yourself a passport. A passport is required to visit Europe—no exceptions. Don't put off applying for your passport to the last minute because it takes four to six weeks for the government to process the application (the times are longest right before summer). The application fee is $135. You also have to supply your own passport photos, which costs about $10 at Walgreen's, CVS, Wal-Mart, etc. You can save that cash by printing your own passport photos. Visit epassportphoto.com, upload your own photos, and they'll email you a sheet of photos that you can print yourself at Walgreens (or wherever) for $0.15. This is what I do.

If your trip abroad is less than six weeks away, you can pay an additional fee of $60 to expedite the process. This will bring the processing time down to about two to three weeks. You also have to pay for overnight shipping both ways—which costs $20 each way.

Are you leaving in less than two weeks? Shame on you for not planning—but all hope is not lost. You can apply in person at a US Passport Agency and you'll get your shiny new passport in about two or three days. You'll need to make an appointment, prove that you're leaving very soon, and pay an extra sixty-dollar fee. Additionally, there are only a handful of US Passport Agency offices, so you may have to travel a long time if you're not lucky enough to live near one.

If you already have a passport, be sure it will be valid for the entirety of your trip. Some countries might require that the passport be valid for another six months after the end of your trip. Renewals cost $110 and follow the same four to six week processing timeframe as obtaining a new passport.

Visit travel.state.gov for all the details on how and where to apply for a passport.

Visas are not required for most travelers. Normally, Americans need only a valid passport to visit Europe—Turkey, Russia, and a few Eastern Europe countries are the only exceptions. The US Department of State website is the best resource on up-to-date country specific guidelines (travel.state.

gov). Generally, Americans can travel visa-free for 90 days anywhere in Europe and 180 days in the UK. If you plan on traveling for more than 90 days, it gets a little more complicated. Read the section about long-term travel for more details.

Make photocopies of important documents. It's always a good idea to have a few copies of the photo page of your passport. I like to make a few physical copies and a digital copy (email it to yourself). This helps speed along the process of replacing a lost or stolen passport.

Additional Important Pre-Departure Considerations

Call your bank and credit card company before you leave. Let your bank know that you will be using your card overseas. Otherwise they are likely to put a hold on your card or even cancel it the first time you use it abroad since international transactions look suspicious.

Write down important information in a small notebook. Write down your passport number, phone numbers printed on the back of your credit cards, every reservation number you receive, addresses to places you're staying, and anything else you think might come in handy. Having it in a notebook is good because you have easy access to it but always keep an electronic copy, too.

Get foreign currency before you leave. Some travelers like to get a little foreign currency before they leave. Generally, you can count on finding an ATM in any European airport, but some people like the extra security. It's best to get just a small amount of cash from your local bank since they will give you a pretty poor exchange rate.

Book your first night's accommodation. Even for those of you traveling without a plan, you'll still want to know where you're sleeping the first night you arrive. This is especially true if you fly into the UK because you're required to fill out a form stating the address of where you're staying before you'll be allowed through passport control. They are strict about it.

Purchase health and travel insurance. Your normal health

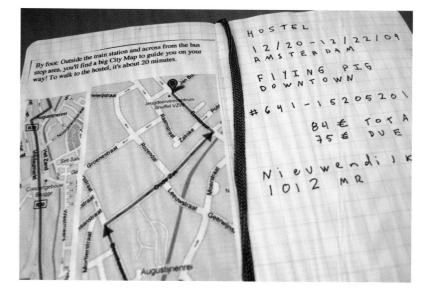

Having important info at your fingertips can be a huge help.

insurance more than likely won't cover you while abroad (check your plan) and don't assume that socialized medicine will be cheap for you because it isn't. That's why travel insurance is a smart choice because you'll still rack up huge medical bills if you need emergency care. And just like most things in life, the more you pay, the better coverage you'll have. Read all the fine print of your policy so you know exactly how much coverage you have. In addition to covering health-related issues, some insurance plans will cover theft, damage of your electronics, trip delays and cancelations, baggage delays, and car insurance.

There are dozens of travel insurance companies so you'll have to shop around and do some research to find the right one for your trip.

Fill medical prescriptions. Stock up any medicine that you require before you leave because it could be tough to get what you need while in Europe. Technically pharmacists will only fill a prescription written by a local doctor, but some might be willing to bend the rules in certain cases. It will be most helpful if you make a copy of your prescriptions.

Break in your shoes. You're going to be walking a ton as you explore the streets of Europe, so break in your shoes before leaving.

Understanding Travel Seasons

There is never a bad time to visit Europe and each season offers something to travelers. The three travel seasons in Europe are high (summer), low (winter), and shoulder (spring and fall). Each season has advantages and disadvantages, but you should choose when you go based on your travel style.

HIGH SEASON

The peak travel time in Europe runs from about mid-June through August. The nice weather and comfortable temperatures bring hordes of visitors—but who can blame them? I love Europe in the summer. The locals are out in the cafés enjoying sunny days, and the farmers' markets have the best produce. There is nothing better than enjoying a nice picnic in a park on a warm summer day.

While European summers are generally comfortable, there are times when the temperature rises and it can be hard to escape the heat. A lot of apartments, hostels, and hotels are not air-conditioned and some public transportation isn't air-conditioned either, so it can

Soak in the lovely summer weather.

19

Look, Mom, no crowds!

get rather uncomfortable when its crammed full of riders.

The hostels are full of young travelers so you're sure to meet plenty of fellow travelers. On the other hand, the best hostels will fill up so it is wise to book in advance. Additionally, Europeans travel a lot during the summer so many of them put their apartment for rent via services like Airbnb.com.

I also like how it doesn't get dark until around 9:30 in the summer. The sidewalk cafés are full late into the night, and you'll find the streets full of people—which adds to the ambiance of the city.

All the attractions are open during the busy season so there is never a shortage of things to do. The summer is also the best time for music festivals and concerts.

However, Europe is crowded in the summer. People are everywhere

and it can be hard to escape the crowds. Popular museums and other attractions will have long lines and you'll continue fighting the crowds once you get inside.

The price of accommodation, transportation, and some attractions are elevated during the summer as well, so your travel dollar doesn't stretch as far.

LOW SEASON

As the temperature drops, so do the crowds and prices. Winter in Europe can be a great time to travel, and it is a totally different feel than visiting during the summer.

Other than around Christmas and New Year's, crowds are virtually nonexistent during the winter. You can walk straight into museums without waiting in line and enjoy the artwork without having to push your way through mobs of camera-touting tourists. I also feel like I get a more authentic look at the culture because I'm not surrounded by tourists. I find that the locals are friendlier because visitors are not constantly bombarding them.

Speaking of Christmas, one of my favorite things about traveling in December are all the Christmas markets all throughout Europe. Additionally, a lot of cities put up ice-skating rinks and other fun winter activities that add to the celebrations.

Airfare to Europe drops drastically in the winter and is often hundreds of dollars cheaper than the summer. Accommodation is another area where you can save quite a bit since hostels, hotels, and rental apartments are desperately trying to get business. You may be able to negotiate some good deals in person if you show up at the end of the day when hotels are desperate to fill rooms.

After spending multiple winters throughout Europe, I know firsthand that weather is hard to predict and changes often—one day it will be sunny and mild and the next it will be downright cold and rainy. To be honest, spending all day outdoors while it's cold and gray can become miserable. Of course, it helps if you dress properly, but you'll never be able to fully escape the cold when it's twenty-eight degrees and damp.

Naturally the weather tends to be nicer in the south but don't expect beach weather. The UK, France, Belgium, and the Netherlands are normally fairly mild but expect frequent light rain. Temperatures drop as you move north and east.

Furthermore, the days are short. The sun sets in Paris around 5 p.m., in Oslo the sun is down around 3:30 p.m. Naturally, it gets a lot colder when the sun goes down, so it makes it more difficult to sightsee comfortably. Most parks shut down at dusk and some sights might have shorter hours.

Small towns, especially ones that cater toward tourists, often turn into ghost towns in the winter. I traveled through Normandy in February and all the small seaside towns were completely closed except for maybe a café here and there. Therefore, it usually makes more sense to stick to big cities in the winter.

Packing also becomes more difficult in the winter because you need heavier and bulkier clothing. This becomes more of a problem when you live out of a carry-on sized backpack, but it's managable if you choose the right types of clothes.

SHOULDER SEASON

In most of Europe the shoulder season runs from mid-September to early November and mid-March to mid-June. These times of year are great because the weather is generally nice but the major crowds haven't arrived yet.

The temperatures during the shoulder season can be very pleasant in much of Western and Southern Europe. Even Eastern Europe can be quite comfortable this time of year. I spent a week in Prague during early April and all I needed was a light

England in early May. Lovely weather and hardly any tourists.

jacket. On the other hand, I've had plenty of chilly days in Paris as late as early June.

Unfortunately prices don't seem much different than summer as more and more people travel during the shoulder seasons. Airfare will be a little cheaper than in the summer but it will be more expensive than the winter. Accommodation follows the same pattern.

Guide to Long-term Travel In Europe

Many people dream of traveling around Europe for months but various visa laws make it much more difficult if your visit extends past ninety days. It is important to familiarize yourself with the different visa laws or you could risk being deported and banned from much of Europe if you overstay. It does take a bit of extra planning but there are still options for determined travelers.

The Schengen Area. Before you start planning your multi-month trip to Europe, you need to learn about the Schengen Area. The Schengen Area is a group of twenty-six countries in Europe that have eliminated passport controls between their shared borders. Basically, you can travel between two bordering Schengen Area countries without having to go through immigration or needing to show a passport. When most travelers mention being able to stay in Europe for more than ninety days, they are generally referring to staying within the Schengen Area—this is because the Schengen Area encompasses most of the countries in Europe.

How the Schengen Area affects you. Americans and Canadians can only stay in the Schengen Area (without a special visa) for a period of 90 days within a 180-day period. If you spend 90 days in the Schengen area during any 180-day period, you must wait another 90 days before you can apply to enter the Schengen area again without a visa. The clock does not "reset" if you leave the Schengen Area before your 90 days are up.

Schengen Area Countries: Austria, Belgium, Czech Republic, Denmark, Estonia, Finland, France, Germany, Greece, Hungary, Iceland, Italy, Latvia, Liechtenstein, Lithuania, Luxembourg, Malta, Netherlands, Norway, Poland, Portugal, Slovakia, Slovenia, Spain, Sweden, and Switzerland.

However, not all European countries are part of the Schengen Area and each has their own rules about how long you can stay without a visa. Notable countries include:

- United Kingdom (England, Scotland, Wales, and Northern Ireland)—180 days
- Republic of Ireland—90 days

- Romania—90 day
- Croatia—90 days
- Cyprus—90 days
- Belarus—30-plus days (need visa but you apply for it in-country. Cost about $35.)
- Ukraine—90 days
- Others—Check the US State Department website (travel. state.gov) for updated requirements for US citizens.

Note: Bulgaria, Croatia, Cyprus, and Romania are prospective members, but their entries have been delayed multiple times so it is unknown when they'll officially join.

WAYS TO EXTEND YOUR STAY PAST NINETY DAYS

Visit both Schengen and non-Schengen countries. The easiest ways to extend your trip past ninety days is to split your time between Schengen and non-Schengen countries. For example, once your ninety days has expired in the Schengen Area, travel to the UK, Ireland, or the many Eastern European countries that aren't part of the agreement. Once you've spent those ninety days there, you are free to return to the Schengen area for another ninety days. You can keep repeating this process until you run out of money.

Working holiday visa. Citizens of Canada, Australia, and New Zealand have working holiday agreements with many European counties that last between one and two years. These visas are intended to allow young people (18–35) to work while they travel. There are a few stipulations, but the visa is relatively easy to obtain. Unfortunately, the United States does not have a working holiday visa program with any European country. However, there is a company called BUNAC (bunac.org) that sells various programs that allow young people to work, volunteer, or intern in Britain and Ireland. The programs last between four to twelve months.

Become a student at a European university. Full-time foreign students are granted visas to complete their studies. There are many university courses taught completely in English throughout Europe (but your options will increase exponentially if you speak the local language). Additionally, a few countries charge foreign students the same tuition as its citizens—which can be as low as a few hundred Euros a year. Once you have a visa, you are free to move around any EU country without hassle. It isn't exactly uncommon for students to pay the super cheap tuition, get their student visa, but just travel and never actually go to school.

There are many full-time foreign language courses throughout Europe that will enable you to get a student visa—this is a nice option if you want to learn a foreign language and travel on the weekends and holidays. These courses normally don't follow the same tuition guidelines as normal European universities so they're more expensive. For example, the intensive twenty-five-hour/week French language course through the Sorbonne University in Paris will cost about $4,000 for a semester. However, student visa holders are often entitled to work twenty hours/ week. There are many options available throughout Europe but you'll have to scour the web.

Long-term tourist visa. Some countries offer a long-term tourist visa generally valid for one year. The process for applying for a long-term tourist visa is complicated and can take months to get approved. I know France is one country that will allow you to apply for a one-year visa; however, you need to have a lot of money in the bank and you won't have working rights. The French consulate never specifies how much money you need to have in savings but most people speculate it's around $30,000. Additionally, you have to satisfy a list of other requirements that a large majority won't fulfill. The French Consulate of San Francisco (consulfrance-sanfrancisco.org) does a pretty good job of keeping information up to date (but requirements seem to change often).

Language assistant program. France and Spain (maybe other countries, too) have English language assistant programs that are run by the government. You normally do need to have some knowledge of the local language, but this is a good way to stay in Europe for a long period of time. I personally know a lot of people who've done a seven to nine-month language assistant program in France. Most language assistants work approximately twelve hours in class each week and get paid around $1,100/month after taxes. Some assistants get lucky and don't have any classes on Monday and Friday—which allow them to travel around Europe on the weekends.

Teaching English as a foreign language (TEFL) jobs. I know some people who were able to get TEFL jobs in Prague and they were granted six-month visas (which could be renewed). You'll need some type of TEFL training, but this could be a good way to stay in Europe for an extended period of time. This is also common in Spain. However, you're on your own to find clients and there is no guarantee that you'll find work.

Self-employment or freelance visa. If you're self-employed and have the ability to work from anywhere in the world then you might be eligible for a self-employment visa. France has a version of this that can be pretty complicated, and I believe you have to get the visa before you arrive in France.

Germany is another country that issues this type of visa for foreigners but you don't apply for it until you get to Germany. Registering as a freelancer is surprisingly simple if you meet all the requirements. You just need to fill out a few forms, prove that you have a decent amount of savings, and you'll get a one-year visa. One of the most popular places to be a freelancer is Berlin since it is cheap (by European standards) and it has a strong start-up culture. Visit this site for information about working in Berlin—http://service.berlin.de/dienstleistung/305249/en/.

European passport. Do your parents (or grandparents/great grandparents in some cases) have citizenship

to a European country? If so, you might be able to apply for a passport for that country. Visit the country's immigration website to see their citizenship requirements. Once you have a passport from an EU country you can live and work in any EU country, without any paperwork or restrictions. This process can take a very long time but it is worth looking into.

Stay illegally. While I certainly don't recommend it, many people just overstay the ninety-day limit and continue to travel. This is mainly possible because there are no border checks between Schengen member countries. For example, if you travel from France to Italy, there is a very minimal chance that anyone will look at your passport—whether you're European or not. There will sometimes be immigration officials on trains but they usually won't look too closely at your passport if you look like an average Western tourist. However, sometimes they do look closely, so do this at your own risk.

The biggest chance of getting caught is when you actually leave the Schengen zone (even if you're going back to your home country) because the immigration officials will often add up the amount of time you've been there.

After living in France for eighteen months, I went back to the United States via Iceland and they questioned why I was in Europe for so long. Luckily, I had my valid French work permit card in my wallet because I had no other proof in my passport that showed I was allowed to stay in Europe that long.

According to anecdotal evidence, Scandinavian countries, as well as Germany, Netherlands, Switzerland, and Poland are all pretty big sticklers about checking the length of time you've been in the Schengen area. Therefore, if you do overstay the limit, I highly recommend you don't leave from those countries.

The countries with the most relaxed immigration checks tend to be France, Italy, and Greece. They sometimes don't even stamp passports of people entering on flights straight from the United States. Additionally, they seem never to look at the passport for outgoing travelers. If you do overstay ninety days, leaving from one of these countries is a safer bet—but just make sure you don't change planes in one of the countries with stricter policies. (See a list in the previous paragraph.) For example, when I flew from France to the United States, I changed planes in Iceland and they checked my passport closely at the airport there.

So what are the penalties if you overstay the ninety days? It seems to vary. You might get a warning and be forced to leave the country right then. Or you might also get a big fine and be banned from entering the EU or any Schengen Area country for one to five years. Honestly, I wouldn't want to risk it.

Purchasing Airfare to Europe

Your plane ticket to Europe will easily be one of your greatest expenses, so it is smart to spend a little time searching for a good deal. Unfortunately, after the economy collapsed, many airlines cut back on the number of international flights so there are fewer tickets available—which means there are fewer inexpensive tickets available. At the moment, expect to pay between $900 and $1600 for a round-trip ticket (from the United States), but you can find cheaper airfare with a little bit of effort and luck.

STRATEGIES FOR FINDING THE CHEAPEST FLIGHTS TO EUROPE

The keys to finding good ticket prices are persistence, planning, and flexibility. Following are some strategies I use for finding the best price on airfare.

Choose your season. The time of year you travel will have the biggest impact on ticket prices—no surprise there. High season round-trip fares (mid - June through August) will typically run from $1,100 to $1,600. Low season fares (mid - November through

Easter) are the cheapest and are generally in the $600 to $900 range—fares do rise around Christmas. Finally, shoulder season rates (mid - September through late November and Easter through mid - June) are normally around $800 to $1,000.

Search multiple departure airports. Airfare can vary drastically based on your departure airport so search all the airports in the area. You'll have to do a cost/benefit analysis to determine if traveling to another airport is worth the potential savings.

Search multiple European airports. If you're flexible about which airport you fly into, there is the potential to save hundreds of dollars. The largest airports (London, Frankfurt, Paris, Madrid, and Amsterdam) tend to have the best prices, but sometimes you can find a good deal by flying into a smaller airport.

Always keep in mind that the cheapest option isn't necessarily the best choice—it has to fit into your travel plans. For example, say you want to visit France but you find a flight into Dublin that costs $200 less than flying into Paris. You'll spend a lot of time and money getting from Dublin to France so you'll negate any potential savings. It would make more sense to just fly into Paris.

Alternatively, Europe does have numerous budget carriers, so you might be able to fly into the cheapest airport and then take a cheap flight to your preferred destination. This does make logistics a bit tougher and it could take a lot of extra time. You'll have to do a cost/benefit evaluation if you choose this option.

Search multiple arrival and return dates. Ticket prices can vary greatly depending on when you travel. Shifting travel dates by a day or two can sometimes save quite a bit of cash. Again, keep in mind that your time is also valuable, so it might not make sense to cut your trip short a day just to save $30.

In general, the cheapest days of the week are generally mid-week because those are the least popular times to travel.

Save time and money with an open jaw ticket. During my last trip, I was able to save about $110 by arriving in Paris and departing from Amsterdam. This is referred to as an "open jaw" ticket.

An open jaw ticket isn't always cheaper than a standard round-trip ticket but if both the arrival and departure airports match up with your travel itinerary, you can save time and extra travel expenses because you don't have to backtrack to your arrival airport.

Search for two one-way tickets. I've had mix results with this technique but buying two one-way tickets can sometimes save you a bit of money. On the other hand, sometimes this method is much more expensive.

Buy tickets in advance. Don't wait until the last minute to book your flight. About ten years ago, you were able to score good deals on last-minute tickets, but this is very rarely the case anymore. Airlines now use super complex algorithms to ensure their pricing strategy fills up their planes. These days, last-minute tickets generally cost twice as much as tickets purchased a month before departure.

The sweet spot for booking a flight to Europe seems to be about four to five months before departure. I'd recommend starting your search six months from when you want to leave and continue to monitor fares. You probably don't want to purchase tickets earlier than six months in advance because airlines generally charge full-fare for these tickets.

Sign up for email alerts and social media. A good way to find deals is through email alerts from various booking sites. They do start to clog up your inbox pretty quickly, though. I recommend opening up a new email account just for these emails—just don't forget to check them every few days. Many airlines also post short-term sales via Twitter so that is another options.

Look at the foreign version of booking site. I discovered this trick accidentally when I was trying to book a ticket from Paris to the United States. I was using Kayak.com but it automatically redirected me to the French Kayak site when I was in France. So I did a search and I found out that the same ticket was $130 cheaper when I booked through the French version. However, you'll have to do everything in the foreign language (which isn't hard with your browser's translator tools). The only potential problem is that you'll have to contact the foreign country's customer service if you have a problem down the road. I tried to call US customer support but they couldn't look up my reservation so I had to do it in French.

Cheap fares are often nonrefundable. If you need to cancel your ticket, you might have to eat the cost, so purchase travel insurance if you're worried. Additionally, some cheap tickets will allow you to change your travel dates but the ticket-change fee can be well over $200 for an international flight. Most travelers don't have a problem, but you should be aware of your ticket's terms.

Willingness to take undesirable flights. Pay attention to your flight itinerary because some discount fares will have super long layovers. It might be worth paying a little extra to not be stuck in an airport for twelve hours.

Look at all fees. Some booking websites will show you the price before taxes and other fees. This is deceptive because all those extra fees will easily add a few hundred dollars to the total price of the ticket. Read all the fine print before you get excited for a super low fare you see online. Also look at the baggage fees because airlines seem to charge more every year.

OUR FAVORITE AIRFARE BOOKING WEBSITES AND RESOURCES

Kayak.com and **Skyscanner.com** are my two favorite airfare search engines, so I always check these two first. Both sites let you search multiple dates and destinations. I've booked 90% of my flights through one of these two sites.

ITA Matrix Search
(matrix.itasoftware.com) is the industry standard flight search engine. It is super powerful and it allows you to do extremely complex itinerary searches. The main drawback is that you can't actually make bookings though the site.

Hipmunk.com utilizes the ITA Matrix software and it allows to you book flights. Hipmunk has a few cool booking features and does a really good job at finding cheap fares. **Google.com/flights** is another site that uses the ITA Matrix software—which was actually purchased by Google a few years ago.

STATravel.com and **StudentUniverse.com** both offer discounted tickets specifically for students and people under age twenty-six. These sites are definitely worth checking out as you can sometimes find a good deal.

Momondo.com and **Mobissimo.com** are two other relatively new booking sites that have started to grow in popularity. Both are worth checking out.

Adioso.com is a great option for flexible travelers. You just type in "New York to Europe" and then choose a time period and trip length.

Then it shows the cheapest option based on your search.

Airfarewatchdog.com will send you weekly email price alerts on specific routes that you choose. It gathers many otherwise unadvertised flight deals and cheap fares. **FareCompare.com, TripAdvisor.com**, and other major booking sites all have email alerts.

You can search the major booking sites like **Orbitz.com, Expedia.com, Travelocity.com, Priceline.com**, and **CheapTickets.com**, but I rarely find the best deals on those sites. Other booking sites are **Vayama.com**, and **CheapOAir.com**

You can often find good deals **directly from the airline's website** so don't forget about them. Sign up for email alerts for all major airlines as they sometimes have short-term deals on airfare that are only advertised through their email list.

Worried that the price of your flight will drop after you purchase it? **Yapta.com** will track your ticket and send you an email if the fare drops. Some airlines will issue you a refund on the difference. Or, if nothing else, you can wallow in agony knowing that you could have paid less for your ticket.

Best Travel Guide Books and Online Resources

Traditionally, guidebooks have been the traveler's bible, but over the past few years the proliferation of online travel resources has greatly reduced the usefulness of the trusty guidebook. And it's no surprise because the Internet solves many of the inherent flaws of traditional guidebooks.

For starters, it takes months to compile a guidebook, so by the time the book is in your hands, much of the information is already two or three years old. During that time businesses go under, cities raise their public transportation prices, restaurants change management, and attractions close down for maintenance—all of which are impossible to keep updated in an annually (or sometimes biannually) published guidebook.

Additionally, in many instances a restaurant or budget hotel will raise their prices (or cut corners) to exploit their newfound fame because they know they'll be overrun with tourists who blindly follow their guidebook's recommendations.

Personally, I only use guidebooks as a backup option when looking for restaurants. I'd much rather find dining recommendations from TripAdvisor.com or local food bloggers/websites. I would very rarely consult a guidebook for accommodation because there are so many crowd-sourced reviews online (Hostelworld.com, hostelbookers.com, Tripadvisor.com, Airbnb.com, etc.).

However, guidebooks do one thing brilliantly; they amass a large amount of information into a single, well-structured format. It is my favorite way to get a feel of the area I'm researching. I can sit down with a good guidebook and learn a lot in just a few hours.

On the other hand, researching on the Internet feels more like you're assembling a giant puzzle—there is no structure, and even after spending hours clicking from link to link, you still don't have a clear idea of what you're looking at. Before you know it, you're reading the complaints that a forty-five-year-old mom from Dodge City has about hotel prices in Berlin. The sheer magnitude of information becomes paralyzing. A guidebook may not feature every little gem, but it provides a solid, fact-checked foundation to your travel planning and then you can use the web to fill in the gaps.

Many guidebooks also provide walking tours, maps, cultural insights, history tidbits, language/translations, and other practical travel information that may not be readily available online. And there is something to be said about the low-tech factor. You can write in a book. You can tear out pages. You can find information quickly and not have to worry about relying on technology.

All in all, I think any good travel planning should include both printed travel books and online guides. Next up, I'll provide you with a list of some of my favorite websites and guidebooks. I strongly suggest going to a bookstore or library and taking out a few guidebooks to see which series you like.

INDEPENDENT ONLINE GUIDES WRITTEN BY LOCALS

SpottedByLocals.com. Having a local show you their favorite restaurants, bars, cafés, shops, and other "under the radar" spots is easily the best way to experience a city—but many of us don't have that luxury. This is where Spotted By Locals shines beautifully. Spotted By Locals is a series of city guides written by handpicked young and hip locals. These guides cover forty-five cities across Europe and they're constantly updated. Each guide comes in PDF format or as an interactive smartphone app. The apps are great because its available 100% offline so you don't have to worry about needing a data plan. Each city guide app costs $3.99 (included free updates for life) and each PDF guide costs €2.99 (updated monthly).

InYourPocket.com. Do yourself a favor and download the free In Your Pocket city guides. These PDF guides cover more than one hundred cities throughout mainly Eastern/Central

Europe and are written by locals that know all the best spots. You can sometimes find printed In Your Pocket guides in hostels through Europe, but they are all available for free on their website.

I like In Your Pocket guides because they provide a lot of practical information about the city (public transportation tips/maps, city maps, money-saving tips, helpful words/phrases, upcoming events, etc.). The guides are updated every few months so the information is current. They're also starting to offer iPhone apps.

Unlike.Net. If you want to know where the hip people hang out, head over to Unlike.Net. These guides are written by culture-savvy journalists, fashion professionals, artists, musicians, and other people way cooler than we'll ever be. You'll find trendy bars, restaurants, shops, concerts and other interesting events. Right now they have about eleven European cities. Unfortunately, most trendy things are expensive, so a lot of things on this site skews toward the pricier side—although there are still some budget friendly suggestions. The city guides can be accessed from the website or via their free smartphone app.

Timeout.com. Want to know what the cool kids are doing? This is the place to go for the inside scoop on hot restaurants, art, entertainment, and shopping.

CROWD-SOURCED TRAVEL GUIDES

TripAdvisor.com. The mecca of user-generated travel reviews for restaurants, tours, and other tourist activities. The reviews can determine the success or failure of a business. It's scary how much power this site has. There has been a bit of controversy over fake reviews, but overall, TripAdvisor is one of my favorite resources when I'm researching a new city.

WikiVoyage.org. This crowd-sourced travel website is the Wikipedia of travel and I use it for every trip. It is the place to check before you visit a location because it provides a wealth of practical information—like the destination's history, transportation system, weather, customs, markets, safety, neighborhoods, festivals, and popular sights. Some articles also recommend restaurants, bars, and hotels/hostels. In true Wikipedia fashion, only expect utilitarian facts and not many opinions (head to TripAdvisor.com for that).

Since it is a wiki-style site, WikiVoyage is edited entirely by volunteers so you don't have the same "quality control" of a professional editor and certain sections might be skimpy, but overall this is an excellent resource—especially for major destinations.

TRADITIONAL GUIDE BOOKS

Wander into any bookstore and you'll find a plethora of guidebooks. Each series is written for a different audience—e.g., students, budget-minded, history buffs, baby boomers, high-end, etc. The books I recommend generally skew toward the budget traveler.

Guidebooks are heavy, so you don't want to travel with more than one or two. Some travelers will cut

out the important pages and make their own personalized guide.

These days, most guidebooks are also available in electronic format. This is a great weight saver but it does come with some drawbacks. First, quickly skimming a physical book is simple but it is a huge pain with ebooks—especially when some of these books are 2,000-plus pages. Travel guide publishers haven't quite figured out how to quickly jump among different sections of an ebook so the user experience can be frustrating. Next, some ereaders don't handle graphics well, so the maps become useless. However, each year e-guidebooks are becoming better and more user-friendly. Here are a few popular guidebooks series:

Lonely Planet. You can't spend more than five minutes in a hostel without seeing a Lonely Planet guidebook. This series has long been the top choice for backpackers and budget travelers, and their 1,300-plus page "Europe on a Shoestring" guide is very popular for those taking a grand tour of Europe. Conversely, many travelers have lamented that Lonely Planet has slowly started moving away from budget and toward more mid-range recommendations—but the series is still an excellent choice.

Lonely Planet publishes a range of books that cover just about every country, region, and major city in Europe. Overall, you can't really go wrong with Lonely Planet guides. However, these guides have become so popular that the places featured in their guidebooks will inevitably become overrun with other Lonely Planet readers.

Rick Steves. If there were one name synonymous with traveling Europe, it would be good ol' Rick Steves. You probably know him as the slightly dorky travel show host on public television. In addition to his travel shows, he also publishes a range of solid guidebooks. I really like that he is a huge proponent of independent travel and experiencing Europe like a local. His books are casually written and give a personal narrative of his recommended sights/restaurants/hotels/etc. Additionally, his books are updated yearly so there is a better chance of accurate information. His audience tends to be athletic shoe–wearing American baby boomers, but his books are still very much appropriate for any budget traveler.

Rick Steves has all sixty-six of his PBS travel shows available on Hulu.com for free (US Only) and he has posted a ton of clips on Youtube. They're great for travel inspiration.

Let's Go. First published in 1961, *Let's Go* was the first travel guidebook specifically for the ultra-budget travel/backpacking niche.

Let's Go has always been researched, written, edited, and managed entirely by Harvard University students, so this guidebook series is still popular with the college-age crowd. If you're looking to pinch pennies and party, this series is probably your best bet.

Rough Guide. These guides are geared toward budget travelers, similar to Lonely Planet, but have a little more cultural and historical information. The reviews tend to be accurate and honest (i.e., they don't sugarcoat their opinions).

DK Eyewitness Guides. The main strengths for the Eyewitness Travel Guides are their top-quality color photography, illustrations, and maps. Plus, the information is brief and easy to read. I find these great for daydreaming about traveling and for planning. I'm not sure if I would bring it along on a trip, but I would read through these at the bookstore as I was researching my trip.

Fodor's and Frommer's. Both these guides offer good information but they tend be to written for a more middle-aged audience.

CHAPTER TWO— PACKING

There is an old axiom about travel from a 1949 *Reader's Digest* that says "Take half as many clothes and twice as much money as you think you'll need for any vacation." While cliché, this advice still rings true and travelers continue to struggle with the concept of traveling light. I've seen backpackers with bags so heavy they can barely stand. You don't want to be this person, trust me. This chapter will talk about everything you need to know about packing—from finding the perfect backpack to helping choose the right pair of socks.

Benefits of Packing Light

Ask any veteran traveler and they'll all endorse traveling light. First, it allows you to travel more freely and easily. You might not realize it now, but you're going to encounter crowded public transportation (usually with lots of stairs), bustling cobblestone streets, small trains/planes, narrow hallways and staircases, tiny hostels, and other difficult travel situations that make traveling with a lot of stuff extremely difficult and stressful. When you travel light, all those obstacles suddenly become less daunting.

A great example of not packing light.

The ultimate goal for packing light is being able to fit all your stuff into a single carry-on piece of luggage—this generally translates to a 45 lbs to 50 lbs backpack. First, it will save you any checked bag fees that many airlines now impose. Next, you never have to worry about the airlines losing your luggage—which is a huge nightmare if you move locations often. If you can't limit yourself to a carry-on sized backpack, I highly suggest at least staying under 60 lbs.

You should also consider keeping the weight of your fully packed backpack under 22lbs (10kg). If you exceed this, you run the risk of exceeding the carry-on weight limit for many budget airlines. Even if you don't plan on taking planes, I still suggest keeping your weight around 20lbs for general comfort.

STAYING FASHIONABLE WHILE ON THE ROAD

I know that a lot of travelers become obsessed with trying to dress like the locals. Relax. It's going to be okay. First, you have to accept the fact that you're never going to be as fashionable as a fashion-conscious local—especially when you're living out of a backpack. Unlike you, they're not spending hours on their feet as they explore the city. If they were, they too would trade their uncomfortable dress shoes and nice clothes for something more sensible.

On the other hand, thanks to the globalization of fashion, Americans and Europeans are pretty much purchasing their clothes at the same chain retailers, so what you see being worn on the streets of London and Paris is pretty similar to what you'll see on the streets of New York and Chicago. Just like in the United States, you'll find H&M, Zara, Mango, Gap, Levis, American Apparel, and Nike stores in just about any major European city. If you want some more inspiration about European style, check out the website of the famous French department store Galeries Lafayette (galerieslafayette.com). It's all in French and the clothes are fairly upscale but a lot of the fashion is geared to the hip twenty-something crowd.

The main point is that you shouldn't freak out too much about fashion because we all kind of dress alike already—the differences are subtle. However, there are a few general guidelines that will help you not look like a complete tourist.

Avoid athletic apparel. Americans have a love affair with wearing athletic clothing in all situations. Wearing gym shorts and athletic tops will automatically make you stick out as an American tourist.

No sweatpants. This is Europe—not your 8 a.m. History 101 class. Avoid sweats. Not only do they look sloppy, but they're also too bulky to travel with anyway.

No running shoes. There is a strong stereotype about Americans and their love of white athletic shoes.

If you're worried about fitting in, then you'll want to leave the running shoes at home. However, a pair of fashionable casual sneakers is perfectly acceptable. Nike, Puma, New Balance, and Adidas all have options that are fashionable and functional. On the other hand, don't sacrifice comfort for fashion because your life will be miserable if you don't treat your feet well while traveling.

It's all about the fit. People assume Europeans look great because they have closets full of designer clothes but this isn't completely true. They may have a few higher-end items but they shop at H&M, Zara, Mango, Gap, Topshop, and other multinational shops just like the rest of us. The secret is that they purchase clothes that fit well—and if the fit isn't quite right, then they'll get their clothes tailored.

Keep it simple. Europeans keep their wardrobes simple and classic. They choose timeless pieces that don't scream for attention. Then they'll add a bright accessory (scarf, shoes, jewelry, etc.) to bring the outfit together. You really can't go wrong with wearing all black and gray.

Flip-flops are for the beach. Sandals are perfectly fine but you should only wear flip-flops to the beach.

Baseball caps. You will see a few Europeans wearing baseball caps but they are mainly teenagers trying to imitate American hip-hop culture.

Avoid hiking clothes. Go to any hiking and camping store and you'll find a lot of high-tech performance clothing designed for outdoor activities. These clothes are durable, lightweight, and quick drying; however, they are ugly and look completely out of place in an urban environment. Although, if you're more concerned about function then this style of clothing might suit you well.

There is some good news. Companies are finally starting to take notice that travelers want fashionable clothing made of these durable performance fabrics. This apparel niche is still in its infancy so the options are limited and the prices are high.

How to Minimize Clothing

The bulk of what's in your bag will be clothing, so if you want to lose the weight you need to minimize and be smart about what you pack. Below are some guidelines to help you pack light.

Mix and match for versatility. The key to being fashionable and packing light is choosing items that are versatile. You'll only bring a few different pieces, but you'll mix and match different items to create multiple outfits.

Everything you bring should look good when paired with any other article of clothing you have. For example, you should be able to blindly pull any top and bottom from your bag and they should look good together. If you can't do this, then you should probably reconsider what you've chosen.

Dark solid colors or simple patterns. Dark colors and simple patterns do a good job at hiding stains and they're easiest to coordinate. Plus, most Europeans tend to wear darker colors, so you have the added benefit of blending in better with the locals.

Bring low maintenance clothing. Make sure the items you bring don't have special washing instructions since you'll be washing your clothes at laundromats. Furthermore, your clothes are going to go through a lot more abuse than normal while you travel so ensure the fabrics you choose are sturdy enough to withstand some punishment.

Forget the "single use" items. That super cute dress or nice slacks you'll only wear once should be left behind. Instead, bring items that can be worn in multiple situations. A good guideline is that if you aren't going to wear it at least three or four times, then you shouldn't bring it.

Add accessories. A nice scarf, fancy belt, or another fun accessory is a simple way to add a little variety to your outfit.

Bring a smaller backpack. You can only bring as much as your bag can hold, so force yourself to bring less by buying a smaller backpack.

Shop as you travel. The shopping in Europe is amazing so you can always buy more clothing as you travel.

There is no difference between packing for three weeks or three months. The length of your trip really doesn't have a big impact on how much you pack because you'll do a load of laundry every week or two.

Clothing Packing Guide for Women

Shirt/blouse. Pack a combination of short and long sleeve tops. Make sure to check the average weather for when you're traveling since it will dictate which type of top to bring. Long sleeve shirts are more versatile since the sleeves can be rolled up if it gets warm.

Light sweater/cardigan. Even summer nights can get a little chilly in parts of Europe so it's nice to bring a sweater or cardigan. Layer with a button-up shirt for extra warmth or to create a new outfit.

Dress. Look for a lightweight dress that can be worn casually during the day and can be dressed up for going out at night.

T-shirts and tank tops. T-shirts or tank tops are great for hot days, undershirts, sleeping, and wearing around the hostel.

Dark skinny/straight leg jeans. Jeans are universal and everyone in Europe wears them. Dark jeans are perfect because they look great during the day and they can be easily dressed up for going out at night. Slimmer jeans are always fashionable and are a safe bet.

Trousers. A pair of lightweight cotton trousers is a nice option since they still look classy and they're a bit more breathable than jeans for those hot days.

Skirts. Skirts are great because they're fashionable, comfortable, and take up very little space in your bag. In the cooler months, they can be paired with thicker tights.

Shorts. Shorts work well in the summer and they can be paired with leggings if it's cool outside. Don't forget to bring a pair of comfortable casual shorts for sleeping or wearing around the hostel.

Leggings. Leggings can be layered with shorts and skirts. Plus, they are comfortable on those long travel days.

Swimwear. If you go to the beach then you'll need something to wear.

Clothing Packing Guide for Men

Button-up shirt. Long sleeve button-up shirts are the most versatile option when it comes to shirts. You can roll up the sleeves when it's warm or keep them rolled down for added warmth. Plus, they look nicer than a standard t-shirt. I only pack casual button-up shirts because it's rare to find yourself in situation where formal attire is required.

Sweater. Lightweight sweaters are nice for dressing up or for cool nights. For maximum versatility, make your sweaters and button-up shirts coordinate because you can wear them together. If you're traveling in the middle of summer, it might be wise to save space by not bringing a sweater.

T-shirts. While button-up shirts are more versatile, I still pack a few trusty t-shirts. They are good for around the hostel, sleeping, wearing under other shirts, and for sightseeing around town on hot days. Lightweight merino wool t-shirts are my favorite because they're breathable and you can wear them a few times without washing because they naturally repel odor. However, they are expensive so they're more of a luxury than a necessity.

Jeans. In my opinion, a pair of well-fitting dark jeans are the best pants for traveling in Europe. Dark jeans match everything, they're comfortable, and they're easy to dress up for a night out. Plus, denim is extremely durable and they can be worn for weeks at a time without needing to be washed.

Some hardcore travelers don't wear jeans because they are fairly heavy and take forever to dry. While it's true, I still think the benefits of jeans heavily outweigh the disadvantages.

Chinos. A pair of well-fitting neutral/dark color chinos is a good option that can be either casual or dressy.

Shorts. In general, men in Europe don't wear shorts, but it is becoming more commonplace. If you choose to bring shorts, stay away from the baggy cargo shorts and choose a more fitted style. You may want a pair of lightweight athletic shorts for wearing around the hostel but wearing them in public will single you out as a tourist.

Swimwear. If you go to the beach then you'll need something to wear. A pair of athletic shorts can always double for a swimsuit.

Socks

The one thing you shouldn't skimp on is the comfort of your feet. Ask any experienced traveler and they'll tell you the importance of quality socks. I know, socks aren't exactly exciting but they truly do make a difference in your comfort.

The best socks are made from fine merino wool and its benefits are numerous. Many of you probably have bad memories of itchy wool, but quality merino wool is soft and comfortable. In addition to adding extra cushioning, wool naturally wicks moisture away from your skin—which keeps your feet dry and blister free. Wool is also naturally odor resistant, so you'll be able to wear a pair of socks a few times before having to wash them (I alternate pairs each day so I don't wear one pair two days in a row). Lightweight wool will air-dry fairly quickly, but heavyweight wool will take a bit longer. And wool isn't just for winter. Lightweight wool is great during the summer and it will actually help keep your feet cool and dry. The major downside is the price, but my socks have lasted a few years—so think of it as an investment.

If you want to save a little money, there is also the option of synthetic (nylon, spandex, polyester, polypropylene, acrylic, etc.) socks. Synthetic materials have many of the same benefits as wool, but they don't perform quite as well. Synthetic will probably dry quicker than wool, but the material does have a nasty reputation of smelling. Some companies treat the fabric with an antibacterial coating, but it still doesn't perform as well as wool.

The one fabric you want to avoid is cotton. While it is the cheapest option, it is also the worst. Unlike wool and synthetic material that wick moisture away from your skin, cotton absorbs moisture and traps it against your skin. This will cause your feet to be chilly and clammy in the cold and soggy in the heat. The moisture will also lead to blisters and unpleasant odors. Trust me, you don't want to be known around the hostel as the person with the terrible smelling feet.

As mentioned previously, socks come in multiple weights and cuts. During the summer, you'll want to stick with lightweight socks, but you could go to a mid-weight pair if you want a little extra cushion for long walks. In the spring and fall, I generally stick with a mid-weight pair. If it gets cold, you can always wear one thin and one medium pair for extra warmth. Finally, in the winter, I prefer heavyweight or mid-weight socks.

No matter what style of socks you purchase it is imperative that they fit well. They should be snug and there should be no movement when you walk, because bunching and rubbing will quickly lead to blisters.

When it comes to socks, my favorite brands are SmartWool, Icebreaker, Wigwam, and Darn Tough (lifetime warranty). These brands all make socks that are 100% wool or a wool/synthetic blend—which means they're generally the most expensive at about $12 to $20/pair. Quality synthetic socks will generally cost $8 to $12/pair.

If you're traveling extra light you just need two pairs, but most travelers will want four or five pairs. Do a quick wash in the sink every few days and you'll be all set.

Underwear

Wash your underwear at night and they're dry by morning.

Another area I don't skimp on when I travel is underwear. Just like with socks, many seasoned travelers avoid cotton. Luckily, there is a new breed of high-performance synthetic underwear that is made for travel and athletic activity. The benefits of quality performance underwear are:

Quick drying. High-tech synthetic material dries extremely quickly so you can wash your underwear at night and they'll air-dry completely in just a few hours. This means you can bring fewer pairs—which will save you space in your bag. For reference, a pair of cotton underwear can take more than twenty-four hours to air-dry (and even more in high humidity climates).

Breathability. Normal cotton underwear is fairly breathable but it still holds in sweat. This leads to that swampy feeling we've all experienced. Travel underwear allows more air circulation and it also wicks sweat away from your body. These high-tech fabrics keep you to cool and dry in all conditions. This is a huge benefit for travelers.

Breathability is also just as important during the winter. Remember, you still sweat when it's cold. That sweat will chill you down—even when you are bundled up. High-tech materials will wick the sweat away from your skin and it will help keep you warm and dry.

Odor control. Many of these fabrics have natural anti-odor properties or a special antimicrobial coating. Those benefits speak for themselves.

Lightweight. Travel underwear is made of extremely lightweight material, which means less weight in your bag.

Great at home. Even though they're made for travel, these underwear are so comfortable that they're great for wearing long after your travels are over (which helps justify their price). I know many people who have replaced nearly their entire underwear collection with travel underwear.

The most popular underwear among travelers is the ExOfficio Give-N-Go series of travel underwear. They are super breathable, comfortable, and only take a few hours to air-dry. They offer multiple cuts and colors for both men and women. The biggest downside is the price. Women's styles are generally around $15/pair and men's cost about $20/pair. However, you can usually find them on sale if you spend a little time searching online.

Under Armour is another favorite brand of high-performance underwear among travelers and they are priced similarly to ExOfficio. Other athletic companies manufacture similar performance underwear.

If you don't like the feeling of synthetic fibers, merino wool is a great choice. However, be warned because they are not cheap so expect to pay $35 to $50 per pair. If you choose to go this route, the best reviewed brands are Icebreaker, SmartWool, and Minus33.

Footwear

Ohh shoes . . . why must they be so difficult? This is probably the area where people really struggle. Without a doubt, the number-one priority should be comfort. You're going to spend ten-plus hours each day on your feet and you will be miserable if your feet hurt. That means you'll have to sacrifice a bit in the fashion department, but it's totally worth it. However, that doesn't mean you have to completely forgo all semblances of fashion—but you will have to search a bit.

The solution that many inexperienced travelers choose is to bring multiple pairs of shoes for multiple situations. This is a mistake. Shoes are bulky, heavy, and they take up a lot of precious space. I recommend sticking with a maximum of two pairs. You can maybe get away with three pairs if one is super lightweight and doesn't take up much space. Alternatively, I know plenty of people who travel with a single pair.

You may consider bringing a quality pair of insoles for added comfort and support.

WOMEN'S SHOES

Women have it a little tougher than guys when it comes to choosing which shoes to pack—especially when it comes to fashion. As always, comfort should be top priority.

For your main everyday pair, I suggest a pair of fashionable, yet supportive sneakers. These are what you'll wear as you sightsee. Additionally, a comfortable pair of flats is also a nice option for a second pair of shoes, because they don't take up much space and they can be either dressed up for going out at night or they can be worn more casually. Sandals are another popular lightweight choice for summer travel, but you'll want a pair that offers some support.

If you're mainly concerned about comfort and practicality, then all-terrain waterproof hiking shoes are an excellent choice. These are especially a great option in rainy or snowy conditions so you don't have to worry about wet feet.

But what about that sexy pair of high heels? Honestly, I'd leave them at home. If you do bring a pair, wear them sparingly and make sure they are comfortable enough to walk in. As you're well aware, heels can easily cause blisters, which will continue to haunt you long after that night out. I know plenty of fellow travelers who've chucked their heels after a few weeks of travel.

MEN'S SHOES

Guys have it fairly easy when it comes to shoes. The first option is athletic running shoes. You will stand out as a tourist but you'll keep comfortable. If you're interested in blending in a bit more, then I recommend bringing a pair of fashionable sneakers, because they're both comfortable and stylish enough for a night out. Nike, Adidas, Puma, and most other major shoe companies make plenty of options. If you want to step it up a bit, there are plenty of comfortable casual leather shoes that work well in many situations.

Another popular option for backpackers is all-terrain hiking shoes. While not very stylish, they are extra supportive and they perform great in rainy or snowy conditions. This is probably the best option if you want to ensure the comfort of your feet. However, I generally don't recommend hiking boots because they're too bulky and they're overkill for city travel.

I wouldn't pack dress shoes either because you'll get little use out of them. As a budget backpacker, you probably won't be dining in any fancy restaurants and a nice pair of sneakers will be fine in all but the most exclusive nightclubs.

Finally, be sure to bring a cheap pair of rubber sandals if you stay in the hostels. You'll want them for the showers. Trust me.

Outerwear

Waterproof/water-resistant jacket. The winter, spring, and fall tend to be fairly rainy in much of Europe, so a rain jacket is a nice thing to have. You don't need a raincoat in much of Europe during the summer so I would opt for an umbrella.

There are generally two rain jackets categories—hardshells and softshells. Hardshell jackets are completely waterproof and they're lighter than their softshell counterpoint. The main drawback to a hardshell is its lack of breathability. This means that interior moisture (i.e., sweat) can't escape and it will leave you feeling clammy and balmy.

Some high-end hardshell jackets do have greater breathability but they're expensive.

Softshell jackets are technically only water-resistant (some are virtually waterproof) but they are highly breathable. The fabric is also flexible so it is more comfortable to wear. Additionally, softshells normally provide more warmth and look more casual—so they're the best option for travel.

Fleece jacket. Fleece is a great material because it provides a lot of warmth without being bulky. A fleece can be worn as an outer layer or it can be layered under a rain jacket or winter coat to provide extra warmth.

You never know when it's going to rain.

Additional Accessories

You gotta get a cool pair of shades.

Scarf. Both European men and women wear scarves, so they're a great way to look like a local and they add a little extra style to your wardrobe. You can always buy a few as you travel, as they also make great souvenirs.

Sunglasses. Sunglasses are not only practical, but they're also a way to make a fashion statement. After living in Europe, I noticed that Ray-Ban Wayfarer style sunglasses were a top choice of the truly fashionable.

Winter Clothing

Europe is a big continent and the weather will vary greatly by region. That's why it's important to be prepared for multiple types of weather. For example, January in Madrid sees multiple days in the upper fifties but in Berlin the temperature usually stays below freezing. Thanks to the jet stream, cities on the western coat of Europe tend to be fairly mild but rainy. Winter travel can get pretty miserable if you don't dress properly. This guide will teach you everything you need to know for staying warm and comfortable.

GUIDE TO LAYERING CLOTHING

Traveling during the winter can be a little tough especially since you don't have a lot of space for clothing. In most situations, the best way to stay warm isn't with heavy winter coats or bulky sweaters. The secret is layering multiple articles of clothing. This drastically reduces bulk and it saves space in your backpack.

The idea behind layering is simple. Basically, you wear multiple thin layers and you add or subtract layers depending on the weather conditions.

It isn't rocket science but it is very effective when used correctly.

Base layer

My merino wool base layer keeps me warm without adding bulk.

The base layer is very important. In addition to providing warmth, it wicks away moisture and sweat from your skin (yes, you sweat in the cold) and transfers it into the next layer of clothing where it evaporates more quickly. Base layers need to be worn tight against the skin. They are available in a few different materials:

Merino wool. Merino wool is the ideal base layer material. It transfers moisture and retains heat well. Higher-end merino wool doesn't itch, but it can get expensive. Merino wool is naturally odor resistant, so you can wear it a few days without worrying about getting funky.

Synthetics. Synthetic materials transfer moisture well and they are a good option for many winter travelers—especially since they are less expensive than merino wool. The main downside to synthetic material is its tendency to absorb body odor so they might start smelling pretty bad after a single wearing.

Silk. Silk isn't too popular anymore but it does a good job. Silk can be difficult to care for, so many people prefer the more robust synthetic material or merino wool. It is also fairy expensive.

Cotton. Cotton is popular, but should be avoided. Cotton absorbs a lot of moisture but doesn't wick it away—it just holds damp material next to your skin. This is the complete opposite of what you want in a base layer and it will actually make you colder.

Mid layer

The mid layer is the everyday items that you'd normally wear. Depending on the temperature, it can be a t-shirt, button-up shirt, light sweater, etc. This provides a little extra warmth and can be worn alone if the weather is warm enough.

Insulating layer

The real warmth comes from the insulating layer. Depending on the conditions, your insulating layer may also be your "outer layer." You can wear multiple thin insulating layers to adjust to the temperature. If you get too hot, it is easy to remove layers until you are comfortable (and vice versa). Insulating layers should be a little loose to allow for better insulation. The most popular insulating layer fabrics are:

- **Fleece.** Fleece is as warm as wool but it's lighter and less bulky. It also has the ability to hold in warmth even if it gets damp. A fleece jacket is also versatile because it can be worn as an outer layer on a warmer day or a mid layer on a cold day.

- **Wool.** Wool is a great choice. It has been keeping people warm for thousands of years and it will still keep you warm even if it gets damp.
- **Synthetic (Thinsulate).** It's not as effective as wool/fleece but it is cheap, lightweight, and does a fairly good job at retaining warmth.
- **Down fill.** Down filled "puffy" jackets provide a ton of warmth while being incredibly lightweight. Another nice benefit is its ability to be compressed into a ball the size of a shoe, which makes it amazing for ultra-light travel. The main downside is that it loses all its insulating properties when wet so you'll need an umbrella or an additional waterproof layer if it rains.

Shell layer

The shell layer keeps away the elements (wind, snow, rain, etc.). The shell layer is usually in the form of a jacket and it should block the wind and be waterproof. Ideally, the shell layer lets interior moisture escape (look for jackets that are "breathable"), while not letting wind and water pass through from the outside. There are a multitude of jackets that fit these criteria, but there are no jackets that can be totally waterproof and extremely breathable—there will always be some kind of trade off.

Normally I say that a **heavy winter coat** is too bulky and often unneeded if you're backpacking during the winter. However, if you plan on visiting extremely cold climates, you might consider bringing a heavyweight winter coat. You're going to spend a lot of time outdoors so you might as well be comfortable.

Spending eight hours a day in sub-freezing weather calls for a heavy coat. And a hat. And a scarf.

WINTER ACCESSORIES

Socks. The importance of quality socks has already been covered but they are crucial in the winter. Pack a few pairs and bring an extra pair while sightseeing in case your feet get wet.

Hat. A good hat makes a huge difference when you're traveling during the winter. Wool and fleece are the best materials.

Gloves. You probably don't need bulky ski gloves but a nice pair of gloves does wonders on a cold day. I suggest thinner gloves or those "mitten-glove combo" things so you can still use your camera without having to take your gloves off.

Scarf. I found that wearing a scarf really helped keep me warm. There are a million styles/materials, so I just suggest getting one that feels and looks good.

Waterproof shoes/boots. European winters are generally more rainy than snowy so you may consider getting a pair of waterproof hiker-style shoes. Boots are bulky and heavy but they are nice in the parts of Europe that experience deep snow or slushy city streets. Granted, neither boots nor shoes will be stylish, but wet feet will quickly ruin your day.

Useful Travel Accessories

Below are some helpful travel accessories that will come in handy while you are traveling. You don't need to bring everything on this list but I tried to only list the most useful items.

Daypack for daily sightseeing. A small bag or purse is great for miscellaneous things (camera, souvenirs, rain jacket, guide books, etc.). I recommend getting a daypack that isn't too large because a big bag will make your back hurt after wearing it for a few hours.

Fast drying travel towel. A quick drying towel is a must if you're staying somewhere that doesn't provide towels (e.g., hostels or maybe couch-surfing). These towels absorb a large amount of liquid and they can air-dry in a few hours. Travel towels are usually much smaller than a normal towel, so I suggest buying a large or XL size—especially if you have long hair.

Small keychain flashlight. It is always a good idea to have a flashlight when you travel. They're essential if you're staying in hostels because it prevents you from waking everyone in the room when you need to find something during the night. They are also nice for navigating dark streets, illuminating your luggage, or in case of a power outage. I love the Streamlight 73001 Nano Light Miniature Keychain LED Flashlight because it is super small (it fits on a keychain) but it provides a ton of light.

Earplugs and eye mask. An eye mask is nice if you take a lot of planes or trains, or if you stay in hostels (some jerk will turn the lights on at 3 a.m.). Additionally, you'll be glad you brought earplugs if you stay in hostels because you'll eventually share a room with someone who snores.

Journal or notebook. I always carry a small notebook when I travel. They're great for jotting down helpful information (directions, phone numbers, addresses, restaurants, etc.) or keeping track of your spending. Sometimes I'll journal about what I did that day or just write about my thoughts—these honestly make some of the best souvenirs. Hardcovers are more durable and hold up well during the journey. I tend to always choose the classic Moleskine brand of notebooks but Field Notes and Rhodia notebooks are also fine choices. Don't forget to take a few pens.

Travel sleep sheet. I'd like to think that the sheets in my hotel or hostel bed are clean . . . but I know that won't always be the case. If you don't want to take a chance then consider bringing a sleep sheet—which is basically your own personal sheet to protect you from any gross hostel sheets. The cheapest option is a cotton sleep sheet but they can be a bit bulky. Silk sleep sacks are more expensive but they're much lighter, less bulky, and they feel great to sleep in.

Water bottle. It is important to keep hydrated as you travel. A basic water bottle is perfectly fine, but you'll save a lot of space by using a soft-sided bottle that can be rolled up when empty.

Sink stopper. When you wash your underwear and socks in the sink you'll need a travel sink stopper.

Travel laundry soap. Woolite makes small packets of laundry soap that are perfect for doing laundry in the sink. The packets are nice because you don't need to lug around a bottle of detergent.

Flexible travel clothesline. A rubber-braided clothesline is a nice way to air-dry anything you need to wash. The braided clotheslines are ideal because they don't require any clothespins—you just stick the clothes through the braids.

Stain remover. Tide To Go Stain Remover Pens are great for getting stains out of clothes. I used one more than I thought I would have. Alternatively, individually wrapped Shout Wipes also work really well and don't take up a lot of space in your bag.

Padlock. If you're staying in a hostel then you'll need a lock so you can secure your stuff in the lockers.

Retractile cable lock. Retractable cable locks are nice for securing your bag to your bunk or a luggage rack. I mainly used mine on long train rides to secure my bag to the luggage rack. They are not super heavy duty but they will deter a thief from running by and snatching your bag.

Duct tape. You never know when you'll need to patch something.

A neat trick is to wrap the tape around a pencil—which eliminates the need to bring a full roll.

Swiss-Army knife/multi-tool. Assuming you'll check luggage or will always take the train, a Swiss-Army knife is a handy tool to have while you travel. If you want something more robust then look at a multi-tool device.

Travel alarm clock. An alarm clock (or a phone with an alarm function) is essential because you don't want to oversleep for those early morning flights and trains.

Digital luggage scale. A digital luggage scale is great for avoiding those costly overweight luggage fees.

Photocopies of important documents. Make copies (physical and electronic) of your passport and other important documents. I also recommend emailing them to yourself so you can access them from any computer with Internet access.

Resealable plastic bags (multiple sizes). Plastic bags are a great way to store your dirty or wet socks/underwear so they don't get mixed with your clean clothes. It is important to store any liquids in sealable plastic bags in case of leaks. In fact, double bag them. You don't want to be one of the many travelers who discover shampoo covering all your clothes. For a bit of extra protection, I recommend putting your important travel documents/passport in a plastic bag. The large three-gallon bags are nice for storing shoes so you don't get your clothes dirty.

Money belt. A money belt is worn under your clothes and it is a safe way to hide cash, credit cards, and other valuable items from pickpockets. Personally, I don't really like money belts because I find them uncomfortable, but a lot of people always wear one—it comes down to personal preference.

Collapsible umbrella. A quality packable umbrella is handy to have when traveling.

Plastic travel utensils. A great way to save some money is to buy meals from the grocery store but not all shops provide utensils.

Toothbrush cover. I like a clean toothbrush . . . call me crazy. You can find cheap covers but I like the Steripod Clip-on toothbrush sanitizer. It sanitizes the brush using voodoo science. Yeah, science!

Lint roller. Your clothes will pick up a lot of dust and lint—especially in hostels. A lint roller is an easy way to help keep your clothes looking presentable.

Guide books and phrase books. I always do a little research about the cities I'm visiting before I go. A small phrase book is nice if you want to learn a bit of the local language.

Corkscrew/bottle opener. You shouldn't have any trouble finding a corkscrew in Europe, but pick one up before you leave if you can't wait to drink. Also, bring a bottle opener because most beer bottles aren't twist off.

Toiletries

Try to minimize the amount of toiletries you bring because they add a ton of weight. Remember, you can buy pretty much anything once you arrive in Europe.

Shampoo/conditioner/body-wash. Pour liquids into those small travel-sized bottles. GoToob travel bottles are some of the best.

Non-aerosol dry shampoo. Dry shampoo is amazing for getting your hair ready when you don't have time for a shower.

Toothpaste and toothbrush. I made the mistake of buying a travel toothbrush on my first trip abroad—it sucked. Now I use a normal toothbrush and a toothbrush cover. I did find that dental floss was much more expensive in Europe, so buy some at home.

Shaving stuff. Razors are more expensive in Europe so bring your own. You can buy shaving cream anywhere.

Deodorant. I've found that deodorant in Europe doesn't seem to work as well—maybe it was all in my head.

Lip balm with sunscreen. Nivea makes a lot of great lip balm that's sold all over Europe. But if there is brand you really like, you might want to bring it with you.

Contact lens/solution/glasses. Contact solution is actually a pain to buy and is normally only sold in pharmacies. Plus it isn't cheap. I'd recommend bringing your own if you can or at least enough to get you through a few days.

Makeup. It is best to bring only the basics when it comes to makeup because it is easy to go overboard. Below are some basic ideas, but you can decide on what is important to you.

You can wear minimal makeup but look polished by wearing a strong **lipstick**. You can also use lipstick as a blush so it is a good way to cut the amount of makeup you bring. **BB Cream** is a great "all-in-one" product. It's a moisturizer, contains sunscreen, provides light coverage as a basic foundation, and it evens skin tone. **Mascara** should be changed every three months so this is a great excuse to buy a new bottle. **Cream blush** is nice because you don't need any brushes.

Condoms. Some souvenirs are no fun, so it is better to be safe than sorry. I'd buy them before you go.

Fabric freshener. Your clothes will probably smell a bit funky after a while . . . so travel-sized fabric spray is a good way to stay a little fresher.

Travel-sized toilet paper. You never know when you'll need a bit of toilet paper, so it is good to carry some travel toilet paper as you travel.

Wet wipes/baby wipes. Individually wrapped wet wipes are a lifesaver when you actually need them—and you'll probably need them.

Hand sanitizer. You'll be touching so much dirty stuff all day and you don't want to get sick as you're traveling.

Body powder. It's common to experience chaffing after a lot of walking—especially when it is really hot. There is a product called Anti Monkey Butt that is great for those hot days or Gold Bond powder is another good option.

Foot cream. Take care of your feet because you'll be walking a lot. O'Keeffe's Healthy Feet Cream is fairly cheap and it will keep your feet from becoming rough and cracked.

Cologne/perfume. I like to travel with a bit of cologne or perfume. Don't bring a full bottle because that would add a lot of weight. I suggest picking up a few sample vials—they'll usually give you free ones at department stores or you can buy them online if you're looking for something specific.

First-Aid And Medicine

Only pack minimal first-aid supplies because you can get everything easily in Europe.

Prescription drugs. Ensure your prescription medicine is in its original box and that you have a copy of the prescription. Some countries will check your medicine when you pass immigration, but I've never been asked. Make sure you have enough medicine to cover your entire trip because it could be difficult getting your medicine abroad.

Pain medicine. In many parts of Europe, you can only buy medicine (even basic stuff like aspirin) from a pharmacy. This isn't really a huge problem, but some pharmacies have limited hours (many closed on Sunday) and the prices are usually fairly high, so you might as well have a few pills on you before you arrive.

Bandages. They're nice to have readily available and they're easy to carry. Throw a few in your bag for cuts and blisters.

Motion sickness pills. If you suffer from motion sickness, I'd pack a few motion sickness pills before you leave.

Pepto tablets. Traveling can take a toll on your stomach. Pepto-Bismol tablets are super easy to carry in your bag and they can be a lifesaver. Plus, tablets are much easier to pack than the liquid.

Small pack of tissues. These are helpful for when you look at your credit card bill at the end of your trip.

Guide to Using Electronics in Europe

There is no doubt that electronics play a huge part in our lives, so it is no surprise that electronics have become an essential part of travel. Between smartphones, digital cameras, laptops, e-books, video cameras, blow-dryers, and hair straighteners, the choice of what electronics to pack can get overwhelming. This section will not only explain what electronics are available, but also how to make sure they survive the trip overseas.

EUROPEAN ELECTRICITY BASICS

North America and Europe electronics run on different voltages. North America uses 110 volts and Europe uses 220 volts. How does this affect you? Basically, in most cases you don't have to worry about it because higher-end electronics (laptops, digital cameras, mp3 players, etc.) have built-in voltage adapters so they can handle the voltage differences without any issue. However, low-tech electronics like hair-dryers, curling irons, hair straighteners, etc. don't have a built-in voltage adapter, so they will fry if you plug them into a European outlet because Europe's electrical sockets pump out twice as much voltage.

This device is rated for 100-240V so it's safe to use in Europe.

Your electronics will display the voltage in which your device operates. It will normally be printed near the plug or on the power brick. High-end electronics will usually say something like IMPUT: 100—240V. This means they run on a voltage between 100V and 240V. If the device just says 120V then it won't be compatible.

If your electronic device is only rated for 120V then you have two options—either you can buy a special voltage converter that converts 220V to 110V or you can buy a device that is "dual voltage." The problem with voltage adaptors is that they're bulky, heavy, and they don't always work so there is a chance your devices could still get fried. I wouldn't bother with them.

I would either purchase a dual voltage device (hair-dryer,

55

straightener, etc.) or buy a new device once you get to Europe—that way you'll know it works.

Additionally, North America and Europe use different plug configurations (the UK has their own too). You will need a **plug adapter** to be able to plug your electronics into European electrical outlets. These adapters will NOT have any impact on voltage—they simply convert the plug style. Plug adaptors are fairly cheap, so it's smart to bring a few since you'll probably be traveling with multiple electronic devices.

INTERNET AND WI-FI

Free Wi-Fi is fairly easy to find throughout Europe but you'll find the most options in medium and large cities. Free Wi-Fi is fairly standard in hostels and in a large number of cafés. You'll also find free Wi-Fi at McDonald's and Starbucks (but some require you to purchase something). Most major cities have an Apple Store so you can always stop there to use the Internet on their computers or to connect to their Wi-Fi.

Internet cafés are also scattered throughout most cities but they're starting to disappear, so it might take a little searching. In addition to accessing the Internet, cyber cafés usually have printing capabilities that

you may require if you book tickets to museums or transportation online.

LAPTOPS AND TABLETS

The ultimate travel computer is undoubtedly a tablet—they've completely changed the way people travel. They're ultraportable, lightweight, and easily packable. They're also good for reading electronic guidebooks, reviewing city maps, basic photo editing, watching movies, and a huge catalog of travel apps is available.

If you need a little more functionality than a tablet can provide, then you'll want to consider a laptop. However, laptops do add a lot of extra weight and you'll constantly worry about protecting it from damage. For that reason, I recommend traveling without a laptop if possible. If you do feel like you need to bring one, I highly suggest getting the smallest and lightest one you can afford.

SMARTPHONES, DATA PLANS, AND MOBILE PHONES

Most people already have a smartphone so it's natural you'll want to bring it abroad because they can truly enhance your travels. If you want to solely use it with Wi-Fi, be certain to turn off all data and mobile service. You will rack up a huge bill if you use your home mobile and/or data plan overseas.

The easiest way to get data is by signing up for an international data plan from your mobile phone provider. You'll still pay quite a bit for data—around $20 for 100MB of data. For reference, you can burn though 100MB of data by streaming about twenty minutes worth of Youtube videos so it really isn't very much. However, if you use Wi-Fi 99% of the time and only access your data when absolutely necessary, this option may work for you.

If you want to use data regularly, then the cheapest option would be purchasing a data plan in Europe. To do this, you'll most likely need to "unlock" your phone so it can accept SIM cards from other companies. The problem is that most phones sold in the United States are "locked" to your mobile provider so it won't work if you install a SIM card from another mobile company. It's basically a way for mobile companies to keep you from switching carriers. Contact your carrier to see if they'll unlock it but each carrier has their own policies regarding when they'll unlock a phone.

If your carrier isn't being helpful there are other ways to unlock your phone yourself. Plenty of online services will unlock your phone for free or a small fee but you'll have to search for those yourself.

Once your phone is unlocked, you're all ready to go—all you need is a new SIM card and you're ready to start using your phone. Pre-paid SIM cards can be purchased from any mobile phone retailer and shops are numerous throughout Europe. Some countries require that you show a passport and provide an address in that country (just use your hostel/rental apartment address). The

prices for pre-paid data won't be super cheap so you should still monitor your usage and use Wi-Fi when possible.

Another annoying thing you should be aware of are roaming fees between countries. For example, if you use a French SIM card in Germany you'll get charged an inflated rate. The European Union has passed a law that prohibits this practice within the EU but it won't go into effect until December 2015.

Also, many people don't realize that the GPS function in your phone works without needing to use a data or mobile plan. City Maps 2Go and MapsWithMe are the two best offline city map apps.

Some apps allow you to download city maps via Wi-Fi and then use the GPS to pinpoint your location on the map.

Finally, if you just want a basic mobile phone while traveling, you can easily purchase a simple pay-as-you-go phone for around $20 and it usually comes preloaded with $10 worth of credit. These phones can be found at any mobile phone shop.

OTHER ESSENTIAL TRAVEL ELECTRONICS

Outlet plug adapters. You'll need a few plug adapters for your electronics (UK and European mainland have different plugs).

Travel power strip. We travel with more electronics every year, so power outlets are becoming a hot commodity in hostels and hotels. Don't be surprised to only find one or two power outlets in a hostel room for ten people. A travel power strip is almost essential these days—just ensure you get one with a European plug or bring an extra plug adapter.

Dual voltage travel hair-dryer and straighteners. Standard North American hair-dryers, straighteners, and curling irons won't work in Europe. If you plug one into a European outlet, it will fry since European voltage is twice as much as in the United States or Canada. The safest option is to simply purchase new devices once you're abroad. If you'd rather purchase them before you leave, look for devices labeled as "dual voltage."

E-reader. If you're an avid reader, it's much easier to carry around an e-reader than a handful of books. Additionally, most guidebook publishers now offer their books in electronic format.

Headphones. It's nice to listen to tunes as you travel. There are a lot of downloadable audio guides for cities and museums—which is a great way to learn more about the places you're visiting. I prefer the earbud style headphones because they're super easy to pack away.

I love having music with me when I travel. It really helps pass the time during long train/plane rides. I recommend the iPod Touch because it allows you to take advantage of all the apps, too.

Guide to Choosing a Digital Camera for Travel

Picking the right digital camera can be tricky because you want one that fits your travel style and your budget. My digital camera is one of the most essential items I bring while traveling. Luckily, digital camera technology is so good and there are so many great cameras to choose from . . . sometimes too many. This section will explain all you need to know about choosing the perfect camera for you.

IMPORTANT FEATURES TO CONSIDER IN A DIGITAL CAMERA

Size. There is an old saying that goes "the best camera is the one that's with you." That's why I always recommend bringing a compact camera, because the bigger the camera the less likely you'll want to carry it. I know many people who've brought bulky cameras that take amazing photos, but after a few days they leave it back in the hostel because they're tired of lugging it around for eight hours a day.

Today's compact cameras are so advanced that you no longer need a large high-tech camera to take top-notch photographs. Naturally, if you want the ultimate control over your photos or you're a hardcore photography buff, you'll still probably bring along your DSLR but you may consider a second small camera for day-to-day photography.

Megapixels. Many people assume that more megapixels means better photo quality. This simply isn't true. Even budget cameras come with 10-plus megapixels (which is more than what most people need) Anything higher than 8MP should be fine for the average traveler. The real quality comes from a nice lens and sensor quality.

Fast lens. Lens aperture is measured in f/numbers, such as f/2.0 or f/3.5. You want as low a number as possible. Basically, the lower the number, the better it will perform in low-light situations.

Zoom. Having the ability to zoom is a nice feature. When looking at the camera's zoom capabilities, always look for the optical zoom measurement. The optical zoom uses physical glass to enlarge the image. Ignore the "digital" zoom because they just uses software to enlarge the image but it results in poor-quality pixelated images.

Lens quality. A high-quality lens is one of the things that separate low-quality cameras from high-quality cameras. The best way to find out about the lens quality is by reading reviews.

HD video. High-end cameras can easily take movie-quality video but even cheaper point-and-shoot cameras can give some fairly amazing video.

Wi-Fi and GPS. These features aren't necessary but they're kind of cool to have. GPS is cool because it imbeds the exact location of every photo you take. Then you can sync it up to Google Maps to see where you were when you took the photo. Wi-Fi is also handy because it lets you upload your photos to your computer without having to take out the memory card. Some cameras can sync with your smartphone and from there you can upload your photos to the Web.

CHOOSING THE TYPE OF DIGITAL CAMERA FOR YOUR TRAVEL STYLE

There are three major digital camera categories—point and shoot, DSLR, and micro four-thirds. I've also included a fourth category of smartphone digital cameras since so many people already travel with them. In this section, I will talk about the advantages and disadvantages of each camera category.

Point-and-shoot

A point-and-shoot digital camera is a great choice for lightweight travelers and this is the type of camera I recommend bringing. Thanks to advancements in photo technology, it's entirely possibly to get excellent quality photographs from a camera that can easily fit in your pocket. A decent camera starts around $150 and, for around $300, you will start finding some seriously impressive options.

One of the main benefits of a small camera is the fact that you can easily take it with you wherever you go. Don't underestimate this. It is also easy to stow away in your luggage, and it's easy to protect so you don't have to worry about damaging it as much.

Today's cameras are so good that even untrained travelers can take excellent quality photographs. The high-end point-and-shoot cameras give the user more control of his or her photos and it is very possible to get professional quality pictures.

One of the main drawbacks of a point and shoot is its low-light performance. Low-end cameras produce grainy and pixelated images when the lighting is poor. However, high-end models will perform quite well so all hope is not lost.

The other drawback that plagues all point-and-shoot cameras is the lag that occurs between the time you press the shutter button and the when the camera actually takes the photo. In general, it's worse on budget cameras and a point-and-shoot camera will have lag.

Digital slr (dslr)

Digital SLR cameras are often known as "professional" cameras. A serious photographer will have maximum control over the camera to get the best shot possible. If you know what you're doing, you can get some amazing quality photos—especially if you start getting into using different lenses to match your shooting needs. Depending on the lens, a DSLR will also give you better zoom capabilities. A DSLR performs much better in low-light situations so you'll get much better indoor and night photos. Additionally, the shutter lag is virtually nonexistent, so you can capture action much easier.

The biggest drawback of a DSLR is the size. They are a huge hassle to carry around all time—especially for hours at a time. I know plenty of people who ended up leaving the camera behind because of the inconvenience of lugging it around. Additionally, DSLRs are hard to protect when you're on the move all the time, so you need a nice camera bag—which adds even more bulk.

Don't forget to learn how the camera functions because many people purchase a fancy new camera for their trip but then have no idea how to actually use it. Spend a few weeks getting to know how all the functions work to ensure you get the best photos possible.

Micro four-thirds

Micro four-thirds cameras (sometimes called mirrorless cameras) are great because they're about the same size as a point-and-shoot but they produce image quality very similar to DSLRs. They also give the possibility to add different lenses if you're looking for even more control of your shots. Users moving up from a traditional point-and-shoot will also like the minimal shutter lag.

One big drawback to this style of camera is the price. At the low end, they run about $700 and the price can easily double or triple, but an entry-level DSLR is closer to $350. However, as the technology continues to improve, the prices will continue to become more reasonable and I predict that this style of camera will be the perfect high-quality travel camera.

Smartphone cameras

Smartphone cameras are getting so good that they're killing base level point-and-shoot cameras. Their image quality will never be as good as mid- and high-end point-and-shoot cameras but the quality is still impressive. Additionally, they're impossible to beat when it comes to convenience and snapping photos on the go. Plus, it's super easy to share photos online the moment you take them. Modern smartphones take decent low-light images, but don't expect anything too amazing.

Photography buffs will want to stick to an actual camera but, at the rate the smartphone cameras are improving, I can see how many travelers could ditch their traditional camera altogether—especially if all your photos are going to only be viewed online. And, if nothing else, smartphone cameras have proven themselves to be excellent supplementary cameras.

IMPORTANT DIGITAL CAMERA ACCESSORIES

Memory cards. Don't forget to bring enough memory cards. You absolutely don't want to limit the amount of photographs you take because of limited memory card space. Plus, they're very cheap these days so there is no excuse not to bring a few. On my first trip, I didn't bring enough memory cards, so I had to constantly look for Internet cafés to upload my photos to an online storage account. I wasted a lot of time and money doing that.

External hard drive or online backup. It's smart to always backup your photos. I've seen too many people lose all their photos because of corrupt or lost memory cards. A portable hard drive is the simplest option, but with online storage you don't need to worry about corrupt files or losing your hard drive. However, uploading large amounts of data can take a long time—especially if you don't have access to fast/reliable Internet.

Extra batteries. Extra batteries are essential for long days of sightseeing because you don't have to worry about running out of power. You can buy cheap third-party batteries online that work nearly as well as batteries from the manufacturer but for a fraction of the price.

Choosing the Best Luggage for Your Travel Style

A backpack isn't the only luggage option for traveling around Europe. Some people prefer using rolling luggage. Each option can be viable and this section will give the pros and cons of both options.

TRAVELING WITH A BACKPACK

Benefits of using a backpack

Hands-free travel. Having full use of your hands makes navigating European streets and public transportation much easier.

Easily navigate stairs and streets. Traversing cobblestone roads and myriad stairs are made easy with a backpack. Don't expect to find escalators and elevators in all European public transportation. I've seen numerous people in the Paris Metro trying to lug a huge suitcase up its multiple flights of stairs. It isn't fun.

Comfort. A backpack can actually be pretty comfortable—assuming it fits well and isn't over-packed.

Ease of movement. Walking through crowds and tight spaces is much easier with a backpack.

Easy to store. Hostels usually have personal lockers and a backpack will fit in those fine. Most of the time, a suitcase is too large so you'll need some other way to secure your stuff.

Drawbacks to using a backpack

Airline travel. Between the baggage handlers and the conveyor belts used to route luggage, the airlines aren't exactly known for being gentle on backpacks. Most backpacks have a lot of straps that can get caught on the conveyor belts and sometimes they get ripped off (not fun). I aim to always carry on my backpack to avoid these issues. However, many newer travel backpacks have zip-away shoulder straps that make the bags safe for being checked.

Over-packers. Many travelers tend to pack a lot . . . like way too much. I always try to promote traveling light, but if you find yourself needing to travel with your entire wardrobe, you might want to save your back and just use a suitcase.

Cost. A quality backpack isn't cheap (although there are some nice budget friendly options).

Some people don't like them. Some people just don't like having anything on their backs.

TRAVELING WITH ROLL- ING LUGGAGE

While most budget and younger travelers choose to travel with a backpack, there are still plenty of people who prefer wheeled luggage.

Benefits of wheeled luggage

Not having to carry a bag. Obviously, with wheeled luggage you don't need to lug your stuff around on your back.

Ease of packing/organization. Packing a suitcase is pretty straightforward and it is pretty easy to get to your stuff.

Airline safe. Suitcases are meant to travel well in checked luggage (assuming a baggage handler isn't having a bad day).

Able to pack more. You don't have to be as concerned with weight when you use a wheeled suitcase since you won't be carrying it.

Drawbacks to using wheeled luggage

Public transportation isn't always luggage friendly.

Damn dirty stairs. Stairs are the enemy of wheeled suitcases. Wheeled bags are designed to be wheeled around but they are difficult to carry. I've helped people carry their huge suitcases up four flights of stairs . . . it is terrible.

Broken wheels. European streets can put a beating on those wheels. Once a wheel breaks, you might as well get a new suitcase.

Crowds. Rolling a suitcase around in a crowd can cause a lot of frustration.

Trains. The majority of luggage space on a train is above the seat so be sure you can lift your bag above your head. Most trains do have luggage storage areas but they fill up quickly and you won't be able to keep an eye on your bags as easily.

Streets. Rolling a suitcase over cobblestone is about as fun as it sounds.

Harder to store in hostels. If you're staying in a hostel, be aware that most lockers are too small for standard luggage. There might be other places to store your bag but they probably won't be as safe as a personal locker.

Hands full. You'll always have to keep one hand on your bag, which will hinder your mobility.

Added weight. Wheeled luggage is considerably heavier than a backpack so keep that in mind if you plan to carry.

OTHER LUGGAGE OPTIONS

Another possible luggage option is a convertible wheeled backpack that has both backpack straps and wheels—which allows you to choose how to haul around your bag. Unfortunately, these bags are much heavier than standard backpacks because of the extra frame and wheels. Additionally, they are usually more expensive. Most people who bring this type of bag end up wheeling it around everywhere, so it probably makes sense to save money by sticking with a normal wheeled bag.

How to Choose a Travel Backpack

The most popular choice of luggage for budget travel around Europe is

a backpack—hence why it's called "backpacking Europe." Choosing the right backpack can be confusing and time intensive, but it pays to take your time when choosing your pack. A proper-fitting backpack allows you to travel swiftly and easily, but a poor-fitting pack is like an anchor. This section will explain the different types of backpacks available and how to choose the perfect one for you.

BACKPACK STYLES

There are three main styles of travel backpacks—top-loading, front-loading, and convertible. Each style has its advantages and disadvantages. I tend to recommend front-loading backpacks for most people visiting Europe, but any option would be fine. Take a look at what follows to see which best fits your travel requirements.

Front-loading (aka panel loading)

Front-loading backpacks were designed for travel—as opposed to outdoor trekking. This style of backpack opens up like a traditional suitcase. Basically, they are a cross between a suitcase and a backpack.

Front-loading backpacks zip open for easy access.

Advantages

Easy access to all your stuff. You can simply unzip the zipper and get to whatever you need quickly. No need to totally unpack your bag when you need to get to something.

Extra pockets. Most bags of this style include a lot of extra pockets on the outside of the bag. This is nice because you will have easy access to the items that you use often.

Easy to organize. Packing cubes work very well with this style of backpack, so it makes organizing your stuff so much simpler.

Fewer straps. Panel-loading backpacks don't have as many straps as most top-loading backpacks. This means you won't have to worry about getting them caught on things. This is especially important if you fly a lot since the straps get caught on airport conveyer belts.

Disadvantages

Zippers can break. The zipper is one of the weakest points. Higher quality backpacks use heavy-duty zippers that can withstand more abuse, but zipper breakage is still a concern.

Zippers are less waterproof. Water can get in through the zipper. Most high-quality bags now come with waterproof zippers or you can buy a waterproof rain cover.

Poorer fit. Some people complain that these packs are too wide and less comfortable than top-loading backpacks.

Less advanced suspension system. Front-loading backpacks tend to have a less advanced suspension system. This means that the bag will become more uncomfortable on longer treks. However, some of the more advanced (i.e. more expensive) front-loading backpacks do have advanced support systems.

Top-loading

Top-loading backpacks are designed for mountain/backcountry hikers but many travelers also use them. This

style of backpack has a single opening at the top that is closed by a drawstring and covered by a protective flap. These packs are designed to be worn for extended periods of time so they are more comfortable.

Advantages

No zippers for main compartment. You can hold a lot of stuff in your backpack without worrying about breaking a zipper.

More waterproof. There is less chance of water getting into the bag because there are no zippers.

Lighter. Top-loading packs tend to be a lighter weight to meet the demands of long-distance hikers.

Better fit. These bags are slimmer and fit closer to the body so they feel more natural.

Good suspension system. The suspension system is more advanced in top-loading bags because they

were designed for long treks by serious backpackers, so you can comfortably wear the bag for an extended amount of time.

Disadvantages

Difficult to pack/unpack. Since everything is loaded from the top, it's difficult to access stuff on the bottom of your bag. You basically have to take out everything to access anything that isn't on top. This can be somewhat alleviated if you pack your bag in a specific manner, but it is still a hassle.

Lots of straps. All the straps can get caught and ripped off in the conveyor belts at the airport. Make sure all the straps are tied away.

Less secure. The top of the pack is closed via a drawstring so it is a bit easier to gain access than compared to the front-loading which can have its zippers locked.

Convertible

The convertible backpack is essentially a suitcase with backpack straps that can be zipped away. There is a lot of crossover between convertible and panel-loading packs but the convertible packs tend to have a little less structure. Convertible-style backpacks are a great choice for travelers who like a suitcase but want the option to wear it as a backpack.

Advantages

Packable. These bags are easy to pack/unpack and keep organized.

More stylish. Convertible-style bags are sleeker and more stylish so they blend better into urban environments. Hiking-style backpacks stick out like sore thumbs in a city so you'll look more like a local with this type of bag.

Shoulder strap. There have been many times when I wished I could easily throw my bag over my shoulder and this type of bag is perfect for that.

Disadvantages

Suspension system. Generally, the backpack straps are not as advanced as what you'd find in a traditional hiking backpack so they're not as comfortable—especially if your bag is heavy. Some may have minimal or no padding on the shoulder straps. This style of pack may also lack a waist strap.

HOW TO CHOOSE THE CORRECT BACKPACK SIZE

Packing too much stuff is one of the biggest mistakes that rookie travelers make, and it all starts with buying a huge backpack. A large bag enables you to carry unnecessary stuff but a smaller bag forces you to pack light. I've seen people with backpacks so large and heavy that they need a friend to help them stand.

Remember that you're going to be carrying this bag around for long periods of time. You will be miserable if you can't even handle your own backpack. You'll be throwing your bag up in overhead bins on planes and trains. You'll be walking through narrow train aisles and busy streets. An overbearing bag will quickly become a huge burden and it will negatively impact your trip.

Backpacks are measured in either liters or cubic inches. Most bags range from about 35L (2,140 cubic inches) to more than 100L (6,000+ cubic inches). However, I recommend choosing a backpack that's around 50L (about 3,000 cubic inches). Personally, I wouldn't go over 65L. You can always go smaller, but packing becomes a little trickier once you go under 35L. Although, I know plenty of ultra-light travelers who've traveled for months with a very small backpack, so it is possible.

The size of your backpack doesn't necessarily need to correlate with the length of your trip. You'll basically carry the same amount of gear for a two-week trip, as you will for a four-month trip. The only difference is the amount of times you'll do laundry.

If you want to avoid checking your bag while flying, I wouldn't get a bag over 50L (3,000 cubic inches). I have a 50L bag and it barely fit most budget carrier's guidelines (it may have even been a smidge too large but I forced it to fit their baggage template). In addition to skipping the baggage claim, you'll never have to worry about the airlines losing your luggage—which can be absolutely disastrous on a backpacking trip.

IMPORTANT FEATURES

Listed here are some of the features you should look for when choosing a travel backpack. It's not surprising that the more features a backpack has, the more it will cost, so if you're on a tight budget you'll have to make a few sacrifices.

Internal frame. Most travel backpacks have an internal frame made of metal or a lightweight composite material that gives the bag structure. Bags that don't have an internal frame will be less comfortable.

Quality materials and construction. Your backpack isn't going to take a huge amount of punishment but it still needs to be tough enough to withstand airports and being thrown around a bit.

Comfortable shoulder straps. Quality shoulder straps will make your journey much more comfortable and your shoulders will thank you. Look for padding thick enough not to cut into your shoulders. Also make sure the shoulder straps don't pinch your neck because that means the bag doesn't fit correctly.

Adjustable shoulder straps. The most comfortable backpacks have shoulder straps that can be adjusted in multiple places. Additionally, load lifter straps and sternum straps offer further adjustment to ensure a comfortable fit.

Stowable shoulder straps. The ability to stow away the shoulder straps behind a zipped panel is a great feature if you plan on checking your bag while flying. This prevents the straps from getting ripped off or damaged from the airline's conveyor belts.

Padded hip belt. A padded hip belt is very important because it distributes much of your backpack's weight onto your hips—which relieves a lot of back and shoulder pain. This is an area where many cheaper bags cut corners.

Lightweight. Be cautious about the weight of the empty backpack. Some heavy backpacks can weight 7-plus lbs alone so once you start adding clothing, the weight will skyrocket. An extra pound or two truly makes a difference. Luckily, backpacks are becoming lighter every year, but you're always going to pay a premium for the lightest weight bags. Ideally, you'll want a bag that is 3 to 5lbs.

Quality zippers. I prefer backpacks with waterproof zippers. The zippers should also have a little area for a small lock.

Outside pockets. While not a total deal breaker, a few outside pockets are really handy for storing stuff that you need to access quickly.

Back ventilation. Backpacks sit right up against your back and the limited airflow causes a nice sweaty back. Some packs offer a ventilation bubble (or chimney) by using mesh to allow air circulation. This is more of a luxury than a requirement.

Color. Most bags come in bright colors, but I prefer darker colors. This is just personal preference. Some people say that bright colors make you stand out more, but anyone hauling around a large backpack is going to stand out—regardless of color.

Cost. Quality backpacks start around $100 and go past $300—although there are plenty of quality options under $150. If price is a concern, ask your friends if they have one you can borrow, check eBay for used backpacks, or check discount online retailers that sell last year's models.

HOW TO FIND A CORRECT FITTING BACKPACK

It is essential that your backpack fits properly, because a poor-fitting pack will quickly become uncomfortable. Once you find a backpack you like, visit the manufacturer's website to see their sizing information—most will give you a detailed fitting guide.

Get fitted in person. Ideally, you should try on backpacks in person. However, this isn't always possible since local stores may not carry a wide selection of backpacks. If this is the case, you should buy online from a website that has free return shipping.

Get the proper size backpack. Backpack sizes are based off your torso measurement—not your height. Some backpacks are adjustable and some come in multiple sizes. Hip belts are adjustable so they should fit most people, but some brands offer different sizes for people who have a hard time getting a standard belt to fit.

Packs for women. Many brands are starting to offer packs designed especially for women. I know Osprey and Deuter both make women-specific models.

Try on multiple packs. Each pack is designed differently, so you should try on as many as you can.

Weigh down the pack. A quality outdoors store will have weights (sandbags) to help simulate carrying a load in your pack. It is important to try out a weighted pack so you can really know what it feels like.

Packing Aids and Organization

Living out of a backpack or suitcase can be frustrating—especially when you move locations every few days. Constantly packing and repacking everything is not only annoying, but it also leads to wrinkled clothing. Fortunately, there are methods to make it a little less painless. In this section, you'll find advice on how to correctly pack your backpack so you can find everything you need as easily as possible.

PACKING CUBES AND PACKING FOLDERS

The biggest annoyance of living out of a backpack is gaining access to the contents of your bag. Having to pull everything out of your backpack to reach something at the bottom of your pack is one of those things every traveler hates. That's why organization is essential. I've found that packing cubes and packing folders are a great way to keep all your stuff as organized as possible.

Packing cubes help keep clothes organized.

A **packing cube** is simply a small lightweight mesh cube/container that you pack your clothes in. There are different sized cubes and you generally pack clothing groups in separate cubes. For example, pack all your socks and underwear in one cube and t-shirts in another. This makes it easy to know exactly where to find whatever it is you're looking for.

To get the most out of packing cubes, you need to learn how to roll your clothes. This is really simple and it will cut down on wrinkling. For tops, place them face down, fold arms back so it looks like a long rectangle, fold lengthwise, and roll up. This same technique can be done on skirts, underwear, and other garments. I prefer to pack pants, button-up shirts, and sweaters with packing folders because they do a better job of preventing wrinkles.

ORGANIZE YOUR TOILETRIES

A toiletry bag is essential for keeping all your toiletries contained. Bring a toiletry bag that can be hung

up because you'll rarely have much sink space in tiny European bathrooms. You also want a bag that is easily portable because hostel showers will be located a good distance away from your room.

Don't expect to have any counterspace for your toiletries.

Your goal should be to pack light so you shouldn't have a ton of toiletries. I suggest buying a few travel-sized bottles for your liquids/gels because they take up much less space than full-size bottles. Plus, carrying a full bottle of shampoo/bodywash/etc. is going to add a lot of unnecessary weight to your bag.

MORE PACKING AIDS

Plastic bags come in handy for storing dirty or damp clothing. Store your extra pair of shoes in a plastic bag to help keep your clothes clean. I bring various sizes of plastic bags (quart-size, gallon-sized and a few "shopping" bags). Some people use **plastic compression bags,** but I find them to be more trouble than they're worth. Plus, they encourage people to pack more than they need. However, **cloth compression sacks** are great for carrying dirty clothes and they make a nice bag for laundry day.

Minimalist Travel

If you want to take traveling light to the next level, you should consider minimalist travel. The goal of minimalist travel is more than packing light—it's a philosophy. It's about the freedom of only bringing the bare minimum while you travel. This style isn't for everybody and it takes a lot of self-discipline, but it can be extremely rewarding.

ULTRA-LIGHTWEIGHT BACKPACK

The size of your backpack determines how much gear you can bring so the first step in minimalist travel is finding a small pack. The maximum backpack size should be no larger than 50L but serious minimal travelers choose a backpack that's around 25L to 45L.

If you want to take it to the next level, you can seek out backpacks that are specially designed to be ultra-lightweight. Osprey, Granite Gear, and GoLite are three brands that manufacture extremely lightweight backpacks that weigh anywhere from 1.5lbs to 2.5lbs. For reference, most standard travel backpacks weight around 3.5lbs to 5lbs. Additionally, most ultra-lightweight packs will be top-loading because they're designed for outdoor hiking.

MINIMIZE CLOTHING

Minimizing clothing is the biggest challenge of ultra-light travel because you're forced to pare down your wardrobe to the bare essentials, so you need to find items that work well in multiple situations.

First, you can easily wear a pair of pants for a week without needing to wash them. In fact, you can easily travel with a single pair of pants for an entire trip. If traveling in the summer, consider also packing a pair of lightweight shorts.

For day-to-day sightseeing, a nice solid-color merino wool or synthetic t-shirt will suffice. Wool is great because it naturally resists odors, but synthetic materials don't perform as well—you'll just have to wash more often. You don't need more than two or three shirts. In addition, bring a casual button-up shirt that looks nice enough for going to bars or restaurants but don't bring anything too dressy.

When it comes to shirts and pants, it is super nice to have fabrics that are durable, lightweight, and quick-drying. Unfortunately, most clothing made from these fabrics are designed for hikers and outdoorsmen—which means they're kind of ugly and they look out of place in urban environments. However, there is a new breed of fashionable performance clothing starting to hit the market. Three brands making strides in this area are Outlier (outlier.cc), Outerboro (outerboro.cc), and Bluffworks (bluffworks.com). This new fashion-forward performance clothing does tend to be pricy but they're built to last.

For cool weather, a fleece jacket works well to provide warmth. However, serious minimalists travel with lightweight down jackets. These jackets only weigh a few ounces and they do a great job keeping you warm. Additionally, they can be compressed into the size of a water bottle so it can easily fit into your backpack without taking up much space.

A rain jacket is optional and you probably don't need one unless you're spending a lot of time in notoriously rainy climates. Nearly every outdoor company produces lightweight jackets and it's amazing how light and packable some of them are. For example, the Outdoor Research's Helium II jacket weighs in at a trivial 6.5oz. Marmut, Montane, Patagonia, Arc'teryx, REI, and a handful of other companies make quality waterproof jackets that weigh in the range of 7oz. to 14oz.

I generally don't cut back much on underwear and socks since they don't take up too much space in the first place. Many minimalist travelers swear by their ExOfficio travel underwear and only bring two pairs for their entire trip. I bring three or four pairs but that's just personal preference. If you're disciplined about washing socks every night, you can get by with two pair but I bring four or five pairs.

Most minimalists only bring one pair of shoes so make certain they're comfortable. A pair of travel sandals can also be nice since they don't take up much space and they're comfortable in hot weather.

MINIMAL ELECTRONICS

It's easy to be a minimalist when it comes to electronics, but there are really only two things you need to bring—smartphone/tablet and a camera. If you really want to cut down, you can probably forgo the camera in favor of a smartphone with a nice camera. Personally, I'd still bring a compact camera because the photo quality is much better.

Most electronics can be charged via USB, so bring a travel power strip that has USB ports. This way you can leave the power plugs to your devices at home and charge everything though USB.

TOILETRIES

It's commonsense, but you really don't need that many toiletries and anything that you forget you can easily buy on the road. Just bring the basics—toothbrush (with brush cover), toothpaste, deodor-ant, shampoo, and bodywash. I pack my liquids in a handful of travel-size GoToob containers. If you're bringing makeup, only pack the essentials. All your toiletries can be packed away in a plastic bag or you can use a toiletry bag—whatever you prefer.

ULTRA-LIGHT ACCESSORIES

Opt for a **travel towel** instead of a bulky bath towel because it will save a huge amount of space in your bag. Do purchase the large or extra large ver-sion because the small and medium sizes are too small to really be useful.

A **keychain flashlight** will always come in handy. The Streamlight 73001 Nano is a favorite among trav-elers because it's super small but incredibly bright.

That's all you really need to travel. I do encourage you to look through the regular packing list to pick other items you may want to bring but ev-erything else is extra.

CHAPTER THREE— ACCOMMODATION

Between hostels, couchsurfing, rental apartments, and cardboard boxes under bridges, there are plenty of budget accommodation options in Europe. It's wise to learn about each option because there are many creative ways to cut back on your expenses.

Hostels—Beer, Bunk Beds, and Breakfast

Hostels are the most popular type of accommodation for budget travel in Europe. They're inexpensive, located in every European city, and full of other young travelers. Hostels are fairly uncommon in the United States, so most Americans are totally clueless about them and have a lot of misconceptions (I know I did). This section will cover everything from hostel basics to tips for choosing a great hostel.

HOSTELS 101

Hostels—sometimes called "youth hostels"—are the bastions of budget travelers. They are like hotels except the rooms (dorms) are filled with enough bunk beds to house anywhere between four and forty people. You're only renting the bed so you'll share the room with a group of fellow travelers. Obviously privacy is limited, but the low cost and thriving social scene more than make up for the negatives.

Most hostels have multiple options for the type of dorm rooms available. Nearly every hostel has a few private rooms (usually with one or two beds) but all have dorms of various sizes. For example, a hostel could have four rooms that hold eight people, five rooms that hold twelve people, and eight rooms that hold eighteen people. Many hostels also have female-only rooms, but most dorms are unisex.

Cost. A bed in a hostel will cost anywhere from $8/night (in Eastern Europe) to $50/night (big cities in Western Europe). The price depends on the size of room you choose (the cheapest beds are in the rooms with the most people), the location of the hostel, the amenities, and competition from other hostels in town.

I normally paid about $25–$35/night on average in Western Europe and $15/night in Eastern Europe. Keep in mind that I *always* opted for the cheapest room available.

However, hostels quickly lose their value if you want to rent a private room; the price skyrockets. Expect to pay anywhere from $90 to $200/night for a private room and sometimes you still have to share a bathroom and deal with loud people in the hallways. For that price, you can find a decent budget hotel or even a pretty nice private apartment via Airbnb.

Why stay in a hostel? Hosteling is the best way to meet a large group of interesting people from all over the world. It's great because you'll be surrounded by like-minded travelers that all share the love of adventure and a love for having fun. Hostels are also often located in the heart of the city, so you're close to all the action.

Who stays in hostels? You'll find a wide range of people stay in hostels. Most are young travelers between 18 and 30 (some hostels only allow guests between 18 and 35 years old). I've also met really cool seventy-year-olds who are traveling throughout Europe for months at a time. You'll truly meet people from all over the world.

CHARACTERISTICS OF A GOOD HOSTEL

There are a lot of great hostels in Europe and there are just as many terrible ones. I've compiled a list of characteristics that you should keep in mind when searching for a hostel.

24/7 reception. Every hostel has a check-in desk—this is where you pay, get your key, and receive all the important information about the hostel. Some will provide city maps or other practical travel information. Some hostels don't have 24/7 reception and it usually isn't a big deal . . . until your train/flight is late and you try to check-in after reception closes. Now you're stuck looking for a new hostel.

Every hostel room is unique.

Dorm room configuration. Hostel dorm rooms are almost universally filled with multiple *squeaky* bunk

beds. (I've even seen three-level bunks.) Dorms can range from small rooms with two bunk beds to large rooms with twenty-plus bunks. From my experience the most common rooms usually have four to six bunks. The cheapest rooms have the most people, so expect to pay more if you want a room with fewer strangers/snorers. Most rooms are unisex, but plenty of hostels offer female-only rooms.

Don't forget to bring a padlock.

Security. Each hostel has its own version of security. Some require a key/buzzer/secret knock to enter the building. Most hostels at least require keys to enter the dorm rooms.

Nearly all dorm rooms have lockers. These are usually located under the bed but some rooms have cabinet-style lockers in the room. You normally have to supply your own lock. I lock up any valuables and leave my backpack on the bed. I've never had any problems with theft—besides, no one wants a bunch of dirty clothes.

The hostel will probably have a room to store your luggage for when you first arrive (if your room isn't ready) and when you're checking out.

These rooms can range anywhere from a locked storage room monitored by CCTV to an open area on the floor with a pile of bags.

Showers and bathrooms. Hostel bathrooms can be super nice or really terrible. Each hostel has a different set-up when it comes to the showers and toilets. Much of the time, each room has its own bathroom. This means the room of eight people could be sharing one small bathroom. Some have large community-style bathrooms with a few sinks and multiple private shower stalls. Some showers require you to push a stupid button every thirty seconds for the water to work and some are operated by pulling on a chain. I've even stayed in a hostel where you had to walk through the kitchen and through the outdoor courtyard (not fun in the winter) to get to the shower.

The absolute worst are the shower/bathroom combo. I want to dance on the grave of the person who thought this was a good idea. Basically, there is no separation between the shower, toilet, and sink. The entire room gets wet and this is a pain in the ass trying to get dressed when every inch of the room is covered in water.

It's easy to meet fellow travelers at hostels.

Lounge/chill-out room. The better hostels have comfy lounge rooms where people can go chill out and meet other travelers. A lot of these rooms will have a large TV with DVD player, books, board games, big couches (which are often adorned with hungover Australians). This is a great place to meet other people, exchange travel stories, and make plans for going out. This is also where you'll find all the people with laptops checking their social media.

Kitchen and dining room. A hostel with a nice kitchen is a godsend. I try to exclusively book hostels with kitchens—even if it costs a little more—because you can save so much money by cooking your own meals. Hostels with nice kitchens are also much more social, as it gives people a chance to really interact with each other. A great way to make friends is to organize a meal and have everyone chip in a little cash. I think I met all my best travel friends in the kitchen.

The best kitchens have everything you'll need to cook a meal; stoves, ovens, microwaves, refrigerators, sinks, utensils, cups, plates, and pretty much anything else you might need. Don't expect any kitchen to be super clean because they get a lot of use, and the hostel staff usually doesn't enjoy cleaning kitchens.

Breakfast (free). Most hostels have free breakfast. Don't get too excited because it's usually pretty meager—but it's free, so whatever. Just about every breakfast consists of generic corn flakes, white or wheat bread (with jam, peanut butter, some yummy chocolate spread, or butter), orange juice, milk (room temperature), tea, and coffee. If you're lucky, you'll get a croissant. I've been to a few hostels where the breakfast isn't free and it usually costs a lot for what you get.

The hostel bar often has the best deals in the city.

Hostel bar. If you want a hostel with a lively social scene then search for one with a bar. The beer prices at hostel bars are usually affordable and sometimes it's the best deal in town. Plus, drinking in the hostel is safer than wandering the streets drunk after a big night out, and you don't need to worry about getting back to your hostel.

The bars do get a bit noisy, so you might want to book a hostel without a bar if you're a light sleeper—or don't enjoy drunk people.

Free Wi-Fi/computers. Free Wi-Fi is fairly standard in hostels. Most hostels have computers with Internet access, but there is usually a charge to use them. Some hostels have free computers with free Internet but there is usually a long wait to use them since they're always occupied.

Washing machines. If you're a long-term traveler a washing machine is a great luxury. Hand washing your stinky socks (and trust me, your socks *will* stink) isn't fun, so having a machine do all the work is a miracle. Some hostels charge to use the machines, but many don't. The biggest problem is fighting for a machine that isn't being used since most hostels only have one or two washing machines.

Good location. The location will have a big impact on your hostel experience. Obviously, it is much more convenient if you're located near the sights, bars, clubs, grocery stores, and public transportation. Hostels that are farther away from the sights are normally cheaper, so you'll have to decide what is more important.

HOW TO FIND A GOOD HOSTEL

Finding and booking a hostel is incredibly easy thanks to the Internet. The two biggest sites are HostelWorld. com and HostelBookers.com, but there are a few other sites like Hostels.com, Hostelz.com, and Hihostels. com. These sites are great because they allow you to read past reviews of other travelers so you can judge the quality of the hostel before you book it.

I mainly book with Hostelworld. com or HostelBookers.com (they don't charge a booking fee) because they are the two largest sites, and they have the most hostel reviews/ community base. Hostelz.com actually compares reviews and prices from all the major booking sites so they're a great place to search for reviews. Additionally, they pay real travelers to review and take photos of hostels so they're a helpful resource.

When searching for a hostel, simply enter your travel information and the site will give you a list of results. Each hostel is rated by fellow travelers, so you'll get a good idea of if the hostel is worth booking. You can also see videos, pictures, amenities, and directions. You book your reservation by paying 10% of the total payment (by credit/debit card) and then you pay the remainder of the payment directly to the hostel when you arrive. It's super easy.

Once I've entered my travel dates and location into the booking site I dive deeper into the results. I prefer to first filter by rating to see the best rated hostels. But you should also look at the number of reviews because some hostels might have a really high rating but only have a few reviews. I'd rather book a hostel with a slightly lower rating but with a few hundred reviews than a hostel with higher reviews but only ten to fifteen reviews.

Then I look a little closer at the reviews. Most sites break down the reviews into six categories: character, security, location, staff, atmosphere, and cleanliness. You'll have to decide which categories matter the most to you. Be sure to read the written reviews of past travelers, as they can put a story behind the guests' reviews. By doing a little homework, you can find some truly amazing hostels.

MORE HELPFUL HOSTEL TIPS

- The lowest price isn't always the best deal because the hostel might be cheap for a reason. Always compare the price and rating because it's probably worth spending a little extra money for a vastly better experience.
- You might be able to save a little money if you book directly with the hostel because this way the hostel doesn't have to pay a commission on the booking. You can always call to see if they have rooms available before trekking there only to find the hostel is full.
- Write *detailed* instructions for how to get to the hostel from the train station/airport/wherever you're coming from. Getting lost sucks and some hostels can be tough to find.
- Book hostels ahead of time during the busy season—*especially summer*.
- Bring earplugs and a sleeping mask. There will be one person who snores super loud when you're in a room of twelve people. And there will be some jerk who turns the light on at 4 a.m. He'll probably brush his teeth and leave the water running the entire time, too. And I bet he hates puppies.
- Be wary of hostels that allow children under eighteen

because these are often overrun with middle-school kids on class fieldtrips.

- I prefer to stay in hostels that don't rent to stag/hen parties (bachelor/bachelorette parties) as these groups often get belligerently drunk and loud.

- Read the hostel's policies. Some only accept cash, some have a lockout period (usually between 11 a.m. and 4 p.m.) for cleaning, and some even have a curfew. Also pay attention to their cancelation policy because most will charge you for the first night if you don't give them ample warning and you need to cancel your reservation.

- Some hostels charge for linens. I've never encountered this but I have had to pay a refundable deposit on sheets.

- I've never met a front desk worker who didn't speak at least fairly good English.

- Many hostels have pub-crawls and the guides know where to get the cheapest drinks. This is a great way to meet other travelers.

HOSTEL ETIQUETTE

There are a number of unwritten rules to hostel etiquette and, after spending a few weeks in a hostel, you'll start to pick up on the little annoying/rude things people do. I think most "infractions" boil down to being inexperienced with hostel living, but

there are a few cardinal rules that hostellers should be remember.

Your mom won't do the dishes for you.

Clean your own dishes. Hostels with kitchens are great, but many people just leave their dirty dishes in the sink. This isn't cool. Even if you only use a cup – wash it. It only takes two minutes so there are no excuses.

Pack your crap early. When I have to check out of the hostel super early, I always get everything ready and shower the night before. I make sure everything is packed, and I set out my outfit for the next day. The next morning, I get dressed, stash my sleeping clothes, and I'm out of the room in five minutes. I do my best to keep as quiet as possible. This concept is lost on many people. There aren't as many things as annoying as someone spending thirty minutes loudly packing all their belongings at 5 a.m.

Keep the lights off. Every hostel has that jerk that barges into the room and flips the lights on at 3 a.m. Most rooms aren't pitch black, so just take thirty seconds and let your eyes adjust to the light before finding your bed. Use a key chain flashlight or the light from your phone if you really need light.

No parties in the dorm room. The dorm room isn't for drinking games—it's for sleeping. Almost every hostel has a room for parties. Keep it there.

All is fair after 8 a.m. Rule 37 of the Geneva Convention – Thou shall not get angry at the people packing/getting ready for their day if it is later than 8 a.m. After 8 a.m., people are free to do whatever they please so don't all get pissy because you're hungover.

Plastic bags are annoying. For some reason, the sound of plastic bags is about a hundred times louder from about 1 a.m. to 8 a.m. Every crinkle goes straight to your brain. Unfortunately a lot of people pack all their junk in various plastic bags. Please keep your plastic bag usage time during the day.

Snoring. If you snore, people are going to hate you. Get your own room if you're a crazy loud snorer.

Don't hog the heaters. The radiator is a great place to dry your towel/wet clothes but try not to hog it all day. Conversely, don't just throw people's towels on the floor when you want to use the heater—fold them neatly and place them somewhere.

Keep night whispers to a minimum. Whispering late at night isn't much better than normal talking. This isn't the time to have a deep philosophical discussion.

Alarm clocks. Most people use their phones as alarm clocks. This isn't a problem. But please don't stash your phone somewhere deep in your bag, because scrambling through your bag for five minutes while the alarm goes off is pretty darn annoying. Make sure you put your phone in an accessible location. On a related note—the snooze is prohibited.

Don't hog the bathroom. Get in, get out. Enough said.

Don't eat other people's food. Just because something is in the refrigerator doesn't mean anyone can eat it. Stealing someone's alcohol is a big no-no.

Dirty laundry. I really don't have a problem with people drying their laundry in the room – but keep it confined to your bed. No one wants to deal with your dirty socks hung about the bathroom and across the sink.

Don't confine yourself to your group. Traveling with friends can be great, but make an effort to talk to other people. Make solo travelers feel welcome. Walking into a dorm room to find a bunch of buddies that completely ignore your presence is disheartening, I know from experience.

Share the computers. Just because the Internet is free doesn't mean you can spend all day using the hostel computer. You really shouldn't need to spend more than ten minutes on the computer. Check your email, book your next hostel, and leave.

The front desk staff aren't tour guides. The people at the front desk usually have the best idea about what is going on in the city. They'll be able to recommend the best things to do/see around town. It is helpful to give them an idea of what you're interested in doing. Questions like "what are some cheap restaurants?" or "I'm looking for a fun nightclub, any recommendations?" are a lot better than "So... what things should I do here?" Don't expect them to plan your stay for you.

Couchsurfing

Do you want to truly experience the local culture, save money, and make friends all over the world? Then you should consider Couchsurfing. org. The couchsurfing scene has exploded over the past few years and it is hugely popular in Europe. The service is more than just a free place to sleep—it's also a rare opportunity to experience Europe like an insider.

HOW COUCHSURFING WORKS

Couchsurfing is a network of people that open their homes/couches/ extra beds/floors to other travelers for free and it's organized online via Couchsurfing.org. It has grown to be the largest online hospitality community with millions of members in 237 countries and territories.

First you create an online profile and fill it in with details about yourself. Then you can search through lists of hosts indicating they are willing to host travelers for your travel dates. If you find a host that looks interesting, you send them a message to arrange an agreement that works for both parties.

Hosts in large cities get inundated with requests, so you may have to try multiple people before you get a response.

WHAT ARE THE HOSTS LIKE?

The Couchsurfing hosting community is very diverse. Some host travelers every week. Some host one to ten people at a time. Some will make you meals. I even know of some who may give you the keys to their houses and leave for the weekend. Or you might have a really busy host who can only offer you a bed and nothing else. Some hosts are older people and some are students. Most tend to be open-minded individuals who genuinely want to show off their city to new visitors.

A lot of hosts will give you advice about where to go and what to see. Many times, they'll take you around the city and show you good bars and restaurants.

SAFETY CONCERNS

It is understandable to have some concerns about safety. Couchsurfing. org says 99% of all stays are positive. All the couchsurfers I know have had positive experiences. But you still want to be cautious. Use your instincts. Be sure to check references, reviews from past travelers, and don't forget to read each host's profile.

The most vulnerable travelers are single women. Luckily, there are plenty of female hosts (many of whom will accept only female guests). It is generally advisable to only stay with people who have a lot of references. Make sure you read all their feedback, too. Always have a backup place to stay just in case something goes wrong/doesn't feel right.

Additionally, it's no secret that some hosts use couchsurfing as a way to hook up with travelers of the opposite sex—especially solo travelers. It's normally men looking to hook up with women but the opposite also happens. Don't be surprised if some make advances. After seeing enough profiles, you can start to spot which users are trying to hook up with their guests because their profiles usually read more like a personal ad than a standard profile.

TIPS FOR COUCHSURFING SUCCESSFULLY

Complete your profile. You're not going to get a lot of responses from a partially completed profile. Fill it out honestly and make sure it is up to date. Many hosts will base their decision on what your profile is like.

Host guests first. If you've hosted people yourself, you will have a much easier time finding people that will in turn host you. Couchsurfing is a community, so you should try giving back first.

Don't send mass requests. Hosts hate it when you simply send out an impersonal copy-and-pasted mass email to a bunch of hosts. Carefully read each host's profile and send them a personalized email asking if they would be willing to host you. In fact, look for hosts with the same interests as you. It helps ensure compatibility and you're more likely to be accepted. Also, give them the specific dates of when you're traveling—don't just say "I'm visiting your city in April. Can you host me?"

It's more than a free room. Couchsurfing is not a hotel service, but many new surfers make the mistake of thinking it is. In fact, if you just want a free room, then I don't recommend using couchsurfing. It is about sharing your culture with someone else and creating a sense of community. Hosts really go out of their way for their guests and they don't appreciate people who just want a free couch. This is a big problem in large cities because hosts get inundated with requests so make sure you're doing couchsurfing for the right reasons.

Don't contact hosts super early or last minute. Remember that hosts have their own lives that don't revolve around you. They have to make special arrangements when they have guests, so you want to give them enough time to prepare. Don't wait until last minute to contact them. Also, don't contact them months ahead of time either. I would usually try to send a request about seven to ten days ahead of time.

Search active users. Couchsurfing.org has millions of members. Many people sign up and forget about their profiles. This is why it is smart to filter people based on when they last logged onto the website. If someone hasn't signed on for a few months, there is a good chance they're not an active host.

Hosts have lives. Remember that the hosts have lives, too, and they're not doing this to cater to you. Sometimes things come up and they have to cancel. This is a risk you take as a couchsurfer so always have a plan B.

Bring a small gift. Don't give your host money, but it is nice if you give them a small gift. Wine and beer are always welcome. Small souvenirs from your hometown are popular choices. Don't spend a lot of money but get something that shows your appreciation.

Communication. Make sure you ask about the house rules. If you're looking to party, make it known when you're searching for a host. If you're upfront about it, you're more likely to get a compatible host. Many hosts are young university students, so they live in small apartments. You want to let them know right away how many people are in your group. If they're expecting one person and four show up, it could make the host angry.

Also, find out when is the best time to arrive and stick to that schedule. Try not to be super early or really late. Always contact them if plans change so they know what is going on.

Don't overstay your welcome. A lot of couchsurfers abuse their stays by staying too long. Many hosts are too nice to tell them to leave. Try to limit your stay to one or two nights.

Interact with your host. Make an effort to talk to your host. They bring people into their home because they like the social aspect of couchsurfing. If you never interact with them, they'll feel like they're being used for a free room.

Clean. Always clean up after yourself. Take out the trash. Fold up your bedding and make sure you keep your bags out of the way.

Cook. Cook your own food. Many hosts are totally fine with you using their kitchen but don't take their food. Offer the host whatever you're making. They may decline but it is a nice gesture.

Vouch for your host. If everything went well, be sure to leave positive feedback on the website.

ADDITIONAL CONCERNS TO CONSIDER

CouchSurfing isn't always 100% reliable. Hosts can cancel last minute and it can often be hard to get people to respond to your requests. It takes a lot of time to find a host, especially in large cities where there are tons of other travelers.

Sometimes staying with someone you don't know might limit your freedom. They might require you to be back at a certain time or ask you to leave while they're not home. You also might not "click" with your host and it can be awkward.

Many hosts don't live right in the center of town because it is so expensive. Therefore, the location might be less convenient for sightseeing. Although, this allows you to see part of the city that you probably wouldn't have ever experienced otherwise, so it isn't always a negative.

Even though it's called "couch-surfing" it doesn't mean you'll always be sleeping on a couch. You could get lucky by getting a comfy bed or you might have to sleep on the ground.

I think couchsurfing is a great idea. It gives you the chance to truly meet the locals and to see parts of the city that most tourists never experience. It also gives you the opportunity to meet people on a deeper level and hopefully you'll make life-long friends. And we can't deny that it's a great way to save money. It probably isn't smart to rely on couchsurfing as your only means of accommodation, but it is great option if available.

Short-term Apartment Rentals

I will be the first to say how much I love renting short-term apartments when I travel. Don't get me wrong, the comradery and excitement of staying in a hostel is great but sometimes it is nice to have more space and privacy.

Luckily, there are hundreds of thousands of short-term rental apartments in Europe and the number of rental apartments available grows every year. It is an amazing way to experience living like a local, and in some cases, it can save you money (especially if you're traveling in a group).

ADVANTAGES TO RENTING AN APARTMENT

Save money. The cost of renting an apartment can be very reasonable and costs per person drop considerably when split between two or more people. In fact, the price per person can often be less than what you might pay at a hostel.

For example, I've seen a listing for an apartment in Paris that was across the street from Notre Dame and the rent was $830/week. When split between three people, this apartment only costs each person about $40/night. A hostel bed in Paris will cost anywhere from about $32 to $40—and that is for the cheapest option in a ten-person room.

If you're traveling as a couple and want privacy, remember that even a private room in a hostel can cost $80 to $150/night in Western Europe. For that same price, you can rent a quality studio apartment.

Local living. Renting an apartment is a great way to see where the locals live. You'll be in close proximity to neighborhood bakeries and restaurants. You'll experience the city on a much deeper level.

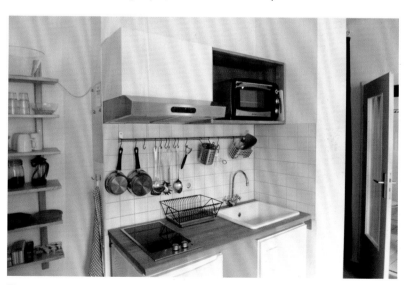

The apartment we rented in Berlin had a great kitchen.

Amenities. With an apartment, you'll get your own kitchen, bathroom, and probably a TV. Many come with free phone and Wi-Fi. You might get lucky and find one with a washing machine.

More relaxed. It is difficult to relax in a hostel because people are always coming and going. Plus, some require that you stay out of your room during the day. With an apartment, you are free to come and go as you please.

DISADVANTAGES TO RENTING AN APARTMENT

Minimum stay. Some apartment rentals have a minimum rental period (usually three to seven days) but this isn't always the case. It'll be rare to find a place that will rent for a single night, so a hotel or hostel would be better for this situation.

No reception desk. If something goes wrong (e.g., there is no hot water or there is a water leak from the apartment upstairs), the owner isn't always available to quickly attend to the problem. Most owners will work hard to resolve the issue, but it isn't as easy as calling down to the front desk.

Possible extra costs. Some rental companies charge extra fees for things like cleaning, safety deposits, and other charges. The extra fees will be listed but don't forget to take them into account.

Rental legitimacy concerns. Most of the time, you're dealing with an individual and many people have doubts about giving a stranger their money—especially over the Internet. I stick to services like Airbnb.com or other established rental sites, so I can read reviews from past guests.

No bag storage. Most rental apartments don't have an area to store luggage once you check out. You may have to store your stuff at a train station or another storage location if you want to spend the rest of the day in the city.

WHERE TO FIND A VACATION APARTMENT RENTAL

Airbnb.com. Airbnb is my favorite rental website, and I've used it multiple times throughout Europe. I've always had great success and the prices really can't be beat. Basically, Airbnb is a service that connects travelers with locals who have spaces to rent. I've always opted to rent the entire apartment, but there are options to rent an extra room or even just a couch in someone's apartment if you're looking to save even more money.

The site is super easy to navigate and booking is super simple. Airbnb also sends their own photographers to take pictures of many of the rental apartments so you know the apartment is legit. Plus you pay for your stay through Airbnb and the money isn't taken from your account until twenty-four hours after you check in. This is great because you don't have to worry about getting ripped off. This would be my top choice if you want to look for an apartment.

"By Owner" rental services. These sites allow apartment owners to advertise their apartment to travelers, so you deal directly with the owner. This option can be a bit risky because you're dealing directly with the owner. However, a large majority are totally legit rental apartments and owners are honest people. Just be sure to read the reviews of past guests. If something doesn't feel right, move on. The most popular websites are VRBO.com, HomeAway.com and Flipkey.com.

Private rental agencies. There are many rental agency sites dedicated to apartment rentals—way too many to list here. Just search for "short-term apartment rental + your desired city" and you'll find a ton of listings. I like to compare the prices of a few different sites because each site will have different apartments for rent. Be sure to do a little research before sending off your money.

Craigslist. Good ol' Craigslist. You'll find tons of people renting their apartments on craigslist. Many of the offerings are posted by rental agencies, but you'll also find individuals renting out their unoccupied apartments. Be very cautious of fraudulent postings, and never send people money if something doesn't feel right. Just use your common sense. Honestly, I'd skip Craigslist, but it's always an option.

Camping

Sometimes you have to get creative when you're on a budget.

When it comes to camping in Europe, there are generally two options—camp in a designated campground or guerilla camping for free in parks, wooded areas, or other hidden away spots.

Campsites are generally located outside the city so the logistics of getting to the campground become difficult if you're relying on public transportation. Some cities do have designated campsites inside the city, but these tend to fill up quickly so plan ahead in the summer. Renting a plot of land for a night will cost around $10 to $20 and most sites will have warm shower facilities,

dining options, and restrooms. Visit http://en.camping.info/campsites to find nearly 25,000 campsites throughout Europe.

Your other option is sleeping for free stealth camping in parks, wooded areas, farms, beaches, and anywhere else you can imagine sleeping. For the average budget travelers this probably isn't a viable option but there is no denying it's definitely a way to save money.

In most cities, it is illegal to set up camp in public but enforcement is infrequent. If you get caught, most police will just tell you to move along once they see you're just a backpacker. The biggest issues you have to worry about are the drunks, drug dealers, territorial homeless people, and a range of nefarious people who typically hang out in city parks at night.

To have the best chance of success it's important to keep yourself out of sight of the public or police by setting up camp at night and packing up your camp before the sun rises. Of course, you'll want to scope out your

Waterproof bivy sacks are a good choice for staying out of sight but it probably isn't super comfortable.

spot before nightfall because finding a place once it is dark will be difficult. Experienced stealth campers also recommend not staying the same place twice.

When it comes to camping gear, most experienced stealth campers bring a quality waterproof bivy sack, a nice sleeping bag, a silk liner, an inflatable sleeping pad, and a rain cover for your bag. This setup is lightweight and low-profile. A travel

hammock used in conjunction with a waterproof cover is another popular choice for camping in wooded areas. A tent isn't ideal because they're easy to spot. Whatever style you choose, it's wise to choose dark colors that will blend into the surroundings.

If you find yourself on private land (farms, people's yards, etc.), you can always ask permission to spend the night. A lot of times, you'll get consent if you look like a sane person or you can check out campinmygarden.com to find people who will let you stay in their yard for the night. Churches are another popular place to set up camp because they'll rarely turn away respectful campers.

Once you've got your gear packed up, you'll need to find a safe place to store it while you're out for the day—most major train stations have luggage lockers that cost around $4 to $8 per day.

Sleeping in Train Stations and Airports

I've slept in a few train stations and airports during my travels through Europe, and I can tell you that they were not pleasant experiences. I wouldn't recommend it as a long-term strategy but it might work in a pinch. Between the cement floors, uncomfortable chairs, and noise don't expect to get much sleep.

Many train stations close around 1 a.m. and the security will kick you out until they open back up around 4 a.m. You should also be vigilant about your belongings because of the heightened chance of theft.

Airports are generally more comfortable and you can usually find a sofa or padded seats. The website sleepinginairports.com reviews nearly every airport in the world and tells you the best places to catch some rest. Sleeping in an airport isn't a good long-term solution since they're located well outside most cities, and you'll have to pay to get there, but it can be an option if you have a super late or early flight.

VOLUNTEER FOR ROOM AND BOARD

Do you have a strong desire to travel but hardly any money? You might want to consider good old-fashioned manual labor in the form of volunteering on farms. The idea is simple—you spend between four to six hours each day (five days a week) doing various farm work (which can range from mending fences and weeding gardens to basic carpentry and tending a vineyard). In exchange for your hard work, you get a free place to stay and all your meals provided.

Most gigs last anywhere from a few days to a few months, and you're not locked into any contract so you can leave if you end up hating your host/work. There are thousands of listings all across Europe so finding another gig isn't too difficult.

Volunteering is a great way to experience a totally different side of Europe that barely any visitors will see. A lot of people also use it as a way to improve their foreign language skills. Whatever your motivation, this is definitely a way to really stretch your travel funds since you'll never have to pay for any housing or meals.

The two most popular organizations are World Wide Opportunities on Organic Farms (WWOOF.org) and HelpX (helpx.net). WWOOF is focused on organic farm opportunities but HelpX has listings for organic farms, nonorganic farms, farmstays, homestays, ranches, lodges, B&Bs, and even sailing boats—so the opportunities are varied. Both services cost about $15 to $30 for a year membership.

CHAPTER FOUR— TRANSPORTATION

Antwerp Central Station—one of the many beautiful train stations in Europe.

One of the truly amazing things about Europe is its vast and sophisticated transportation network. In fact, there are so many options that it can be difficult to know the best option for your travel and budget needs. Transportation is also one area where you can spend a lot of money and waste time if you don't know how the system works. This chapter will tell you everything you need to know to be a savvy traveler.

Exploring Europe by Train

The French TGV train zips across France at 200mph.

Traveling by train is the quintessential method for touring Europe, and rightfully so. It's romantic. It's inspiring. Some might say it's almost magical. And to those of us that don't live in a country where train travel is prominent, it's a little mysterious. Europe's rail network is extremely developed and train service is very reliable—except for the occasional strike. In this section, you'll learn how to plan your journey, how to buy tickets as cheap as possible, and how to make the most of your rail travels.

REASONS WHY RAIL TRAVEL IS AWESOME

Arrive in the center of town. Unlike airports, most European train stations are located right in the center of town. You don't have to spend the time and money traveling into the city because you're already there. Traveling from the airport into the city will usually take anywhere between 20 and 60 minutes and cost $10 to $40.

No long check-in or security lines. There are no lengthy check-in procedures for train travel or security screening. You can simply show up a few minutes before the train leaves, buy a ticket if you don't have one (often from a ticket machine with English instructions), and hop on the train.

No luggage fees. There are no extra fees for your luggage. Just make sure that you're able to lift your bag onto the train.

Bring your own food and alcohol. You can pretty much bring whatever you want on a train—including alcohol. Bring a bottle of wine or a case of beer if you want. You're sure to make a few friends if you give a few away to your fellow travelers.

A vast rail network and multiple trains. Europe's rail network is extremely vast, and it is normally possible to travel to even the smallest towns by train. Most destinations offer multiple trains a day and the most popular routes usually have hourly train service.

Sleep on the train and extend your travel time. If you're traveling a long distance, consider taking an overnight train. These trains have special sleeper cars with bunks. A bunk in a sleeper car will cost about $35 to $55 extra (about the same as a night in a hostel), but you won't lose out on a day of travel. Overnight trains also have normal seats if you don't want to fork over the extra cash for a bunk.

Be spontaneous. Many trains don't require a reservation, so there isn't a need to book ahead. Simply show up at the train station before the train leaves and climb aboard. For trains that do require reservations, the process of reserving a spot only takes a few minutes.

Beautiful views. Europe has a lot of amazing countryside so traveling by train is a great way to see some fantastic views.

Peace and quiet. The train is the perfect place to sit back and relax. There is something very peaceful about staring out the window as you ride silently at 200mph through the European countryside. The train is also a good time to write a postcard to your friends and family, read a book, write in your journal (you'll be glad you did), or continue planning your future travels.

Train travel is comfortable and nearly stress free.

Comfort. Train seats are usually a little larger than plane seats (especially when compared to many discount airlines). You're also free to move about the train whenever you feel like it. Many trains also have seats that face each other and have a table between the seats. These are perfect for groups or if you just like table space. Unless it is a holiday or you're on a very popular route, the train is rarely crowded, so there is a good chance you'll be able to get two seats to yourself.

Reliability. European trains run on schedule well over 90% of the time, but flights are only on schedule around 65%. Most trains will leave exactly when scheduled, so don't be late or you'll miss.

Beautiful train stations. Historically, the train station was the central hub for commerce and transportation. Many European cities showed off their wealth and status by building grandiose train stations. While it isn't a huge deal, it is one of those nice, little perks.

The train is fun. I always found riding the train to be fun. Maybe it is because there are no trains where I live, or maybe it conjures up nostalgic images of riding the train through the Wild West. Whatever the reason, I always found train travel special.

DISADVANTAGES OF RAIL TRAVEL

The costs. Train travel can be expensive. Although there are often discounts for people under twenty-six or if you purchase your tickets well in advance. If you do book in advance, the cheapest tickets are often nonrefundable, so missing your train means you'll need to buy another ticket.

Slow for long distance travel. If you're traveling long distances, it might be smarter to fly. For example, taking the train from Paris straight to Budapest would take around eighteen hours. Therefore, unless you stop and spend a few days in cities on the way, it would make more sense to fly—especially if you're short on time.

Confusion. The train schedules can be a little confusing, especially for beginners, but it is easy to learn. Also, a lot of large cities, and a few small towns, have more than one train station (Paris has six). It's not uncommon to arrive in one station and leave from another. I've shown up at the wrong station a few times, so be sure you read your tickets carefully.

It is also possible to change stations during a single journey. For example, traveling from London to Lyon, France, via the Eurostar. The Eurostar stops at the Paris North station but then you have to travel to the Paris East station to catch the train from Paris to Lyon, because there are no direct trains from London to Lyon. This transfer would require a cheap metro ride.

Rail strikes. Striking is a national pastime in Europe. It happens a few times a year (or more if the people aren't happy), but they plan them in advance so you'll have some time to work out other plans.

How to Plan Your Rail Journey

There are two websites that every train rider needs to know. The first is the German Railway website Bahn.com. On this site, you will find every scheduled train route across all of Europe. All you need to do is plug in your cities and it will tell you all the possible route options and train times—it's pretty amazing. However, you won't be able to purchase any tickets from the site unless the route includes Germany. So once you know the best journey for you, you can purchase tickets from each country's rail network website.

The second site you need to know is Seat61.com. This site has the most in-depth information about traveling Europe via train.

UNDERSTANDING TRAIN TICKET PRICING

Understanding the various pricing structures can be confusing, but it's not too bad once you become familiar with them.

The simplest tickets are for regional and local trains. These trains are slow and they mainly connect smaller towns and villages. The pricing for these trains is fixed so you can buy them at the station and reservations aren't needed or possible.

Similarly, Belgium, the Netherlands, Luxembourg, and Switzerland operate on a fixed pricing system for domestic train journeys. You can purchase tickets online but the only thing you'll save is a bit of time by avoiding the ticket window. However, Switzerland does offer special fares on some routes so spend a few minutes online to see if you can save a few bucks.

Nearly all high-speed and long-distance trains now operate on a tiered pricing structure where the cheapest seats are sold first and the price rises as the departure date nears. Bookings open between 60 and 90 days prior to departure so buy early before the good seats are snapped up. Eurostar tickets can be booked up to 120 days in advance.

Some countries give you the option to buy a seat reservation, but it probably isn't necessary unless it's a super busy route (notably Friday and Sunday night). If the train is super full, you'll still be allowed on the train if you don't have a reserved seat but you might have to stand or sit on the floor—it's rare, but possible.

All overnight trains will require a reservation regardless of the country, but it will be factored into the price of the ticket.

QUICK OVERVIEW— POINT-TO-POINT TICKETS VERSUS TRAIN PASSES

You have two ticket options when it comes to using Europe's rail network—purchase individual train tickets or purchase a rail pass. There are advantages and disadvantages to both methods, but knowing which option is best for your trip can be difficult to determine because there are so many factors to consider.

In general, the cheapest option will be purchasing tickets one to three months in advance. So if you have a set itinerary, this will be the most affordable way to travel Europe by rail. On the other hand, if you want maximum freedom and spontaneity, then a rail pass will almost always be a more economical and practical option than buying individual train tickets last minute.

Again, I want to emphasize that there are exceptions to the advice mentioned in the paragraph above, but it's a good guideline to follow. In the following sections, I'll cover more in-depth details about point-to-point tickets and rail passes, so you can use the information to determine your best option.

PURCHASING INDIVIDUAL TRAIN TICKETS

Buying train tickets can be a little complicated because each country has their own rail system, ticket sales website, and pricing structure. Finding the best price is even more complicated because there is no single website that displays the best

ticket prices for all routes. Therefore, it takes a little work and planning to find the best deal.

The easy way to purchase tickets

The simplest way to purchase tickets online is through RailEurope.com. Rail Europe is a joint venture between a handful of European railways and it was created to sell rail tickets to non-Europeans. Unlike many European rail networks, Rail Europe will mail tickets purchased online outside Europe. You also don't have to worry about difficulties that sometimes arise when paying from a US bank account.

Unfortunately, buying tickets though Rail Europe is more expensive than buying tickets directly through each country's rail network website. That's because Rail Europe does not always display the current travel specials and they charge an extra commission.

Additionally, you can always purchase tickets directly at the train station. The tickets will be expensive if you buy them last minute (unless it's a country that has fixed pricing) and you'll have the potential of waiting in a long line. I once waited well over an hour to buy tickets so buy your tickets early if you can.

The cheapest way to purchase tickets online

As mentioned before, there is no single website where you can find all the best train fares for every train route. To get the best deal, you'll have to go directly to each country's rail operator. For example, when traveling in France you should check the prices at www.voyages-sncf.com.

However, it isn't as simple as it seems. Each country's website has its own rules and quirks that you'll have to deal with. Some sites randomly won't accept US credit cards and others won't mail tickets outside Europe, but you can often pick them up at the ticket window. Sometimes you're able to print them yourself. So when it comes time to book, read the fine print closely so you don't get any nasty surprises. If you book online, ensure you bring the same bankcard you used to make the purchase online because you'll probably need the card to retrieve your tickets.

Booking tickets online in Eastern Europe is tougher/not always possible. It is usually best to purchase them at the station or at a local travel agent. Ask your hostel or hotel and they'll tell you where to locate an agent.

Point-to-point ticket money-saving strategies

Book long-distance trains early. Most high-speed and long-distance trains operate on a tiered pricing system so the cheapest tickets are available far in advance and the prices continue to rise as the departure date approaches. The difference in price is quite drastic. For example, a ticket from Paris to Amsterdam on the Thalys high-speed train is $48 if purchased far in advance, but the same ticket is $180 if purchased a few days before departure. Most

tickets are available for purchase about 90 days prior to departure.

The Eurostar train is the best way to travel from London to Paris, but book early because it can be very expensive.

Eurostar tickets (the train that connects London and Paris) should be purchased as far in advance as possible because the price skyrockets as the travel date, approaches. Tickets are available six months before your travel date and you can save well over $200 by booking early.

In general, train tickets can be purchased between sixty and ninety days in advance so if you have the ability to book early, you'll get the best deals. However, the prices for most of the slower regional and commuter train routes that connect smaller towns and villages are fixed so you simply pay for distance traveled. There is rarely any discount given for buying early, so it's easiest to purchase a ticket at the ticket window or ticket machine.

Split ticketing. Instead of purchasing a single ticket for a long journey, consider purchasing two separate tickets for the same route. It's a little weird but sometimes it works.

For example, you want to go from Paris to Berlin. Along the route, the train will stop at Düsseldorf Station so you would buy one ticket for Paris to Düsseldorf and then another for Düsseldorf to Berlin. Just make sure you buy it for the same route. Sometimes, for whatever reason, this will greatly reduce the cost even though it's the exact same train. It won't always work but it's worth trying.

However, be cautious if you need to change trains where you split the ticket because if your first train is late, then you may be out of luck and miss your second train.

Higher prices for peak travel periods. A lot of rail operators will charge a higher price for the desirable morning and late afternoon travel periods. You can save a little money by choosing a less desirable time.

Youth discounts. Travelers under the age of 26 are often entitled to a fairly hefty discount for train tickets. Indicate your age when booking in person or select your age when booking online. Some countries sell special discount cards for young travelers that can be a good deal if you travel within that country a few times. For example, France's rail service sells a *Carte Jeune* discount card (50€) for travelers ages 18 to 27. This card, valid for a year, gives anywhere from a 25% to 60% discount on train fare. It will usually pay for itself after two round-trip tickets.

Discount cards and special offers. Most countries sell discount cards that can save a lot of money

if you're going to take multiple train trips within a single country. For example, in Switzerland you can buy a Half-Fare Card for about $120 that lasts a month and gives a 50% discount on train fare. Germany has a similar BahnCard. Look for these discounts in any country where you're going to make multiple train journeys.

Some countries also have different discount fare schemes. For example, Germany has the Schönes-Wochenende-Ticket (translated as "Lovely Weekend Ticket") that gives you unlimited travel all throughout Germany on a Saturday or Sunday until 3 a.m. the following day. It only costs about $60 but up to five people can all share the single ticket—which makes it very cheap per person. There is also a weekday version called the Querdurchs-Land Ticket which costs as little as $20 per person if you have five people.

Check websites of all countries on the journey. With international journeys, you can often book a ticket from any country the train passes through. For example, tickets for a train going from Paris to Berlin can be purchased via the French or German rail operator websites. However, the prices may not always be the same, so it doesn't hurt to shop around. Do read the fine print about where you're able to collect the tickets because some countries make you pick up the tickets in the country where you bought them.

Overnight Trains

Taking an overnight train is a popular way to save a little money while also gaining extra travel time since you're traveling while sleeping. You will have to pay a little extra for a reservation on these trains, but you don't have to pay for a hostel that night so it kind of evens out.

If you're on a budget then you can simply sleep in a normal seat. The seats recline a little but enough to sleep comfortably. I know from experience that it's a fairly uncomfortable way to sleep but it's the cheapest option. If you're lucky and the train isn't busy, you can prop your feet up on the seat in front of you.

You also have the option to reserve a small bed in a sleeping car. The most common configurations are six-bed rooms and two-bed rooms. The rooms are small and you'll most likely share the room with strangers unless you're traveling with a group of people. A bed will cost about $35 to $55 extra. You can also rent a cabin with a single bed but expect to pay significantly more.

It is important to realize that many find sleeping on the train to be difficult and uncomfortable because of the noise and constant movement. Don't expect an excellent night's sleep.

Traveling with a Eurail Pass

Personally, I've done trips with and without a Eurail pass. I loved hopping on the train whenever I pleased. I didn't have to worry about planning anything, and I decided where I next wanted to visit on a whim. It's no surprise that one of the most popular ways to travel Europe is with a rail pass.

It's a great option for people who want to see a lot or for those who want the ultimate flexibility. There are rail passes to meet most people's needs. But with so many options, choosing the right rail pass can become overwhelming. This section will cover everything you need to know for making your pass work for you.

RAIL PASS BASIC INFORMATION

A Eurail pass is a single ticket that gives you access to nearly any train in twenty-four countries in Europe

—which includes Austria (including Liechtenstein), Belgium, Bulgaria, Croatia, Czech Republic, Denmark, Finland, France (including Monaco), Germany, Greece, Hungary, Ireland, Italy, Luxembourg, Netherlands, Norway, Portugal, Romania, Slovenia, Slovakia, Spain, Sweden, and Switzerland.

Types of Eurail passes

The **Global Pass** includes unlimited travel throughout all twenty-four countries covered in the pass. The global pass is available in five fixed-length versions—fifteen days, twenty-one days, one month, two months, and three months. This option allows you to travel as much as you want while the pass is valid.

The **Flexi Pass** also covers all twenty-four countries but it gives you the option to choose either ten or fifteen individual travel days within a two-month window. This option is cheaper than the unlimited Global Pass, but it does require a little more planning so you don't waste any travel days.

The **Eurail Select Pass** gives you unlimited travel between three, four, or five bordering countries for five, six, eight, ten, or fifteen travel days within a two-month period (France is not included in this option). This is a good choice if you're sticking to a specific region. The **Eurail Regional Pass** is similar to the Select Pass but it's only valid for two bordering countries. There is also the **Eurail National Pass**, which is valid for a single country (some smaller countries are grouped together into a single pass

—Belgium, Netherlands, and Luxembourg, for example).

The **France rail**, **BritRail**, and **Swiss rail** are country-specific passes that differ slightly from the Eurail National Pass. For example, the Swiss rail pass also includes bus and boat travel in addition to the trains.

Rail pass costs

The price of each rail pass differs, and it's wise to compare each pass based on how much you plan on traveling. You don't want to purchase a thirty-day global pass if you only plan on using the train a few times because you'll end up wasting a lot of money. Additionally, if you're over twenty-six-years-old, you can still buy a rail pass but you're forced to purchase a more expensive first class pass.

The ten-day second-class global ticket is $528, the thirty-day Global Pass is $836, and the three-month Global Pass is $1,453. The ten-day and fifteen-day Flexi Pass is $623 and $817, respectively.

The three-country, five-day select pass starts at $341 and goes all the way up to $736 for the fifteen days five countries pass.

The regional passes range anywhere from $120 to $220 for five travel days and go up to over $500 for ten travel days.

It's also important to remember that pass prices rise each year so visit raileurope.com or eurail.com to find the latest prices. These sites also have tools to help you choose which pass is best for your travel itinerary.

Extra fees for Eurail pass holders

There are a few instances when you'll have to pay extra when using your rail pass. The most common extra fee comes from trains that require a **seat reservation**. Nearly all high-speed trains that operate in France, Spain, and Italy require a reservation, but there are a handful of other routes throughout Europe that also require a seat reservation. Routes requiring a seat reservation are denoted with a "R" printed on the timetable. Reservations can cost as little as $5 but can go as high as $45 for the Thalys train from Paris to Amsterdam. Reservations can be made in person at a train station and some can also be made online or via phone. Additionally, **book your reservation as soon as you can** because most routes only allow a limited number of pass holders to ride the train and they sell out early.

Furthermore, all overnight trains require a seat reservation. Expect to pay $7 to $35 for a reservation in a normal seat. A couchette (basically a bunk bed) can cost anywhere from about $20 to $75 extra. For overnight trains, you'll only use up one of your pass's travel days, assuming your train departs after 7 p.m.

ARE EURAIL PASSES WORTH THE MONEY?

Determining the value of a rail pass is kind of tricky because it strongly depends on your travels so you'll have to do the math based on your itinerary.

A good place to start is to figure the cost per day of travel for the pass. For example, a ten-day Flexi Pass is $623. That means every travel day is worth about $62.

For example, a single ticket from Paris to Berlin would cost around $300 if booked on fairly short notice so that would be a pretty good deal if you had a rail pass. However, Paris to Lille would cost closer to $45 so in that case the pass value isn't that great. Of course, you have to remember that any trip will probably consist of long and short train rides so you want the overall cost of the pass to be less than the individual tickets.

Great for flexibility

Not sure where you want to go? Choosing destinations on a whim? If this is the case, then a rail pass is almost always the best option. All you need to do is hop on the next train. Easy peasy.

Of course, you still want to have some idea of your travel plans because you'll need to choose your rail pass type based on where you plan on traveling. For example, it doesn't make sense to buy a thirty-day unlimited pass if you just visit two or three cities.

Convenience

Let's face it, planning out every stop, racking down the best deal, and then figuring out how to collect the tickets is a pain in the ass. For many people, saving all that time, energy, and stress is worth the extra hundred dollars you might spend on the pass versus individual tickets.

Long distance travel
If you're traveling between multiple major cities, then a rail pass is usually a pretty good deal because those train rides are expensive.

Group travel
Eurail offers "saver" rail passes for groups of two to five who are traveling together. There is only one ticket with everyone's name on it so all riders must ride on the same train but this option can be a good deal if you're part of a large group.

Adult pass costs more
Youths (anyone under twenty-six) get a sizable discount. However, if you're twenty-six or older, you can only buy a first class rail pass. I never understood why there isn't a second class adult rail pass, but them's the breaks.

Not all countries are created equal
Train travel is affordable in Italy, so you'll probably lose money if you spend a lot of time there. The same goes for much of Eastern Europe. However, in the rest of Europe train travel is pricy so a pass makes sense.

MORE TIPS FOR USING YOUR EURAIL PASS
- Don't validate your ticket until your first day of rail travel.
- When using the continuous pass, be sure to plan your trip so you can get the most out of your pass. Start your trip in a country where your pass doesn't work

—England, for example. You can spend a few days in London and then take a cheap flight to Amsterdam. Spend a few days in Amsterdam and then validate your pass once you leave Amsterdam.
- When using a Flexi Pass, don't waste a day of your pass for a short cheap trip. Combine the Flexi Pass with point-to-point tickets to get the most out of your trip. Save your travel days for more expensive trips.
- Plan your trip and compare different rail pass plans. You don't want to purchase a pass that doesn't give you enough travel days, but you also don't want to waste leftover days from a pass that was too large.

HOW TO USE YOUR PASS
Using the pass is simple. The day you want to activate the pass, all you need to do is take it to any train station and an employee at a ticket window will validate it. Now you're ready to jump on a train you desire (assuming it doesn't require a seat reservation).

For the passes that give you a specific number of travel days (Flexi, Select, etc.), you'll write in the date on the pass each day you travel. You need to write in the date *before* the ticket controller comes by to check your tickets or you'll get in trouble. However, some local trains don't always have a ticket controller, so hold off from writing in the date until you see someone checking tickets (just don't let him see you writing on your ticket or you could get fined). You might just get lucky and get a free day of travel.

For overnight trains, you'll only use up one travel day, assuming your train departs after 7 p.m. so don't write in two days on your pass.

Your pass doesn't cover subways, trams, or any other city public transportation (except the Swiss Pass).

WHERE & HOW TO BUY A EURAIL PASS

The two main companies that sell Eurail passes are raileurope.com and eurail.com. There is virtually no difference in price between companies, but sometimes there might be a special so check both websites.

Eurail passes can only be mailed to addresses outside Europe and you can't buy them once you arrive. Additionally, your pass must be validated within six months of the purchase date or it becomes void.

Most companies also offer rail pass insurance. If your pass gets lost or stolen, they'll refund some of your money (check each site's policies). However, the passes can't be replaced without insurance so keep a close eye on it as you travel and treat it the same way you treat cash.

Train Travel Skills

For most Americans, this will be the first time taking a train that's not located in a theme park. The system is actually fairly easy to use once you know how everything works. If you have any questions, don't be afraid to ask employees (most will know some English), other passengers, or simply observe other people.

AT THE STATION

First, make sure you go to the correct train station because most large cities have multiple stations. Even small towns can have more than one, so don't assume you'll leave from the same station at which you arrived. I've done this. Twice.

The information on the departure boards changes often so pay attention.

Large stations can be a little confusing because they'll have multiple platforms. Some even have multiple levels or different sections. Give yourself a little time to find where your train will arrive. Look around for the giant departure board because it will tell you where each train is (or will be) located. It will also give you status updates about any delays, cancelations, or platform changes. Most trains arrive and depart like clockwork. Don't be surprised if it's only in the station for two minutes—so don't be late.

The line at the ticket window can get very long during busy times of the day. Plan ahead if you need to buy tickets.

If you bought your tickets online and you didn't print them yourself, then you'll need to retrieve them. First check to see if you can use the automated machines. Some ticket machines only accept chip-and-pin cards—which is annoying for Americans. If this is the case, you'll need to go to the ticket window. Be aware that the lines at ticket windows can be very long so try retrieving them a day or two before you depart so you don't accidentally miss your train. Additionally, you must bring the same bankcard

that you used to purchase the ticket to be able to pick up the tickets.

Don't forget to validate your ticket or you risk being fined.

If you have an individual ticket, you may be required to validate it before you board the train. Look for a small box (they're usually orange, yellow, or red) with a ticket-sized slot. All you do is stick the ticket into the slot and it will stamp it. If you forget, you could get fined by the train controller when he comes around checking tickets. If you do forget, you'll want to quickly seek out the controller and ask him to stamp it of he'll assume you're trying to ride for free.

When it's time to board the train you can usually sit anywhere unless you have a reserved seat. If you do have a reservation, your ticket will indicate the car and seat number. Train staff will be on hand to assist you.

ON THE TRAIN

Once you board the train, all you need to do is find your seat and store your bag. I prefer to store my bag in the overhead luggage rack. If you're too short to place your bag in the rack, someone is usually willing to help you. Alternatively, sometimes there is storage space behind the seats or between train cars.

Make sure you have your ticket or rail pass ready to show the controller. Sometimes it will take them 10 to 20 minutes before they come by to check tickets. If you need to use the restroom, make sure you wait until the train is moving because the toilet often empties on the tracks. As you start to get comfortable, resist the temptation to put your shoes up on the seat across from you—you'll probably piss off a train employee.

However, the most difficult part of the train journey is knowing when to actually get off the train. I still get confused. The confusion arises because most large cities have a few smaller stations that service the suburbs but the station name will still have the name of the city. So when you stop, you see the city name and assume that you need to hop off. If you do this you'll just have to wait for the next train. As a rule of thumb, if everyone else is still on the train, then it's probably not time to get off. If you're traveling to a major city there is good chance you'll stay on the train until the very last stop. Don't be afraid to ask people around you.

Air Travel Within Europe

Train travel has long been the most preferred and "romantic" way to travel through Europe, but the proliferation of no-frills budget flights across Europe has made flying an attractive option. With the proper timing, you can find insanely cheap airfare throughout Europe.

In fact, this has sparked a long debate (and even more confusion) whether it is better/cheaper to travel by plane or by train. This guide will cover the pros and cons of air travel, the steps you need to take to find the best travel deals, and a list of helpful sites to purchase tickets.

ADVANTAGES TO AIR TRAVEL

Travel long distances quickly. Your time is just as valuable as your money. Air travel lets you travel long distances much quicker than any other transportation method.

Cheap tickets. There are multiple budget airlines in Europe offering no-frills service, so the fierce competition has drastically driven down the price of airfare. I once got a ticket from London to Glasgow for $2 (with all taxes and fees included) through Ryanair—Europe's most popular discount airline. This is fairly uncommon but it is possible to purchase a one-way ticket for $10 to $50 if you book early enough.

DISADVANTAGES TO AIR TRAVEL

Transportation fees to and from airport. The cost for transportation between the airport and the city is another hidden fee many people overlook. Most airports are connected to the city center via trains so the fares are normally reasonable, but this isn't always the case. For example, the train ride from Amsterdam's Schiphol International Airport to the city center is about $6. However, the Heathrow Express (the non-stop train from Heathrow Airport to London) starts at $35. There is also a slower option that costs around $17.

Most airports have a city bus service and a handful of private shuttles that are usually cheaper than the train, but the transportation time is much greater because city traffic is universally terrible

throughout Europe. Additionally, private shuttles often carry multiple passengers, so depending on who gets dropped off first, you could have to wait a long time before you arrive at your destination.

Finally, there is always the option of a taxi. Naturally, the taxi will nearly always be the most expensive option. However, if you're traveling with three or four people, the cost per person might be comparable to using public transportation, and there is the added benefit of being taken directly to your destination. Do a little research before arriving to see the standard taxi fare because there are a lot of crooked cab drivers.

Does anyone like being at the airport?

Time spent at the airport. Spending time in an airport is about as much fun as going to the dentist—especially when you're in an extremely busy one. I know I would rather spend my time seeing the sights than being herded like cattle through a crowded airport. Even though air travel can save a lot of time, it also takes up a lot of time.

First you have to get to the airport (at least thirty minutes travel time—sometimes over two hours). Then you have to get there early so you can check in and go through security. Most airlines want you to check in around an hour before departure. Be aware that some airlines have strict rules about check-in times. I once checked in three minutes too late and they wouldn't allow me to board the flight. I had to spend $100 to buy a new ticket and wait three hours for the next flight.

Security is always fun. It isn't easy keeping track of your shoes, passport, boarding pass, large backpack, and everything else as you pass through security—heaven help you if they ask to unpack your backpack. Once you arrive at your new destination, there is the possibility that you'll have to go through immigration (this can either be quick or take over an hour for some countries). Then you have to spend time getting to your new hostel/hotel. At the end of the day, that 2.5-hour flight turned into a 5 to 6 hour journey.

No pretty scenery. One of my favorite memories from my European adventures is taking the train through Germany. The train rode through a river-valley spotted with small castles and tiny old villages. I would have never experienced this if I flew everywhere.

Extra fees. Many budget airlines charge fees for checked bags (while many major airlines allow you one free checked bag). Each airline has its own fee structure, and if you're not

careful you can end up paying a lot more than expected. The fee structure can be complicated so be sure to double-check the airline's website.

For example, with Ryanair your first checked bag starts at $20 and can cost as much as $60 depending on the weight of the bag. There are also a slew of other small fees for just about everything. Other airlines also charge extra fees so be sure to read the fine print when booking your ticket.

HOW TO FIND THE BEST DEALS ON AIRFARE

Plan ahead and book early. Planning your journey early is one of the best ways to save money, but it takes a lot of time to find the great deals. Airfare is usually cheapest a few weeks in advance of the departure date and the price continues to rise as the departure date approaches. Even a week could be the difference between a $30 ticket and a $120 ticket.

Start looking as soon as you can and continue to monitor the prices until you find a fare that seems reasonable. If you happen to find a limited-time sale, it makes sense to book quickly because the cheap tickets will be snatched up.

The road less traveled is usually more expensive. You will *usually* find the best prices if you fly between the major airports/ hubs. The largest air travel hubs in Europe are **London** (LON: LCY, LHR, LGW, STN, LTN), **Frankfurt** (FRA, HHN), **Paris** (CDG, ORY), **Madrid** (MAD), and **Amsterdam** (AMS).

Fly on the slow days and at slow times. Tuesday, Wednesday, and Thursday are historically the least busy travel days so airlines lower ticket prices to attract customers. Additionally, early morning and late-night flights will be the cheapest.

Travel during the low-season. Airlines lower their prices and have travel specials during the low-season.

Search multiple dates and times. Flexibility is the key to getting a great price. Try searching multiple dates and travel times because a few days can make a large impact on the price.

Search multiple locations. Most travelers have a decent idea of what cities/countries to visit, so search each location and check the airfare for each. Configure your trip around the location with the best prices. Or if you're adventuresome, see where the cheap flights are and travel to those cities on a whim.

Avoid public holidays. There are lots of public holidays throughout Europe and the airlines will jack up the prices to capitalize on the increased demand for flights. This is especially true for long school holidays since entire families are traveling.

Travel light. Many airlines (especially discount carriers) charge for checked bags, so you'll save a lot of money by carrying on your luggage. I used a 50L backpack and it is just small enough to satisfy even Ryanair's stingy carry-on size rules (although it was a very close fit). Just be sure to carefully read each airline's baggage rules.

LOWDOWN ON LOW-COST AIRLINES

No frills on Ryanair.

For cash-strapped travelers, it's hard to find a cheaper way to travel than flying with one of Europe's budget airlines—especially for long-distance travel. Before you break out your credit card, you should learn the ins and outs of traveling with low-cost carriers or you could end up paying a lot more than you should.

There are more than 60 discount carriers in Europe but the big three are Ryanair, EasyJet, and AirBerlin. Don't expect luxury or comfort from any carrier. What you can expect is to get from point A to B for a cheap price.

Pricing and extra fees

Each budget carrier has its own pricing scheme, so it's hard to predict the best time to purchase, but in general it's best to book a few weeks in advance. I'd start looking as soon as possible and monitor the prices until you find a price you think is fair. If the fares seem high then it may be beneficial to wait a few days and check again. Last-minute bookings will usually come at a premium but sometimes you may score a cheap seat if you're lucky—doesn't hurt to check. Furthermore, don't be afraid of cobbling together two one-way tickets as opposed to booking a round-trip ticket because the prices are usually fairly similar.

I've found that you can expect to pay between $60 and $120 for a one-way ticket for flights between major cities if booked in advance. The price might be a little higher if you're flying a long distance or if you're flying to smaller cities. Additionally, some carriers will offer random limited-time sales via their website. This is when you'll find those amazing $10 to $30 tickets. These sales are sporadic but more common during the low season, so you'll have to constantly monitor the websites or sign up for their email newsletter.

However, you need to extra careful about the extra fees that most budget airlines impose because the fees can easily double the price of the ticket. The trick is to follow the rules precisely. Basically, expect that nothing is free. Want to check a bag? Pay up. Want a soda on the plane? Pay up. Want to check in or print your boarding pass at the airport? Pay up. As you can see, the fees can get out of control. Each carrier clearly states their policies on their websites, but it's amazing how many people don't bother reading them.

Other budget airline issues

Most budget airlines, especially Ryanair, are very strict about carry-on size and weight limits. This is one reason I stress traveling light because your bag has to weigh less than 22lbs (10kg) and it has to fit the airline's size dimensions. If your bag is over the weight limit, you'll be forced to make it fit the requirements (i.e., ditch stuff to lighten your load) or pay to check the bag.

You also need to pay attention to the airport location because many budget carriers fly to smaller regional airports located outside major cities. For example, Ryanair claims it flies into Paris but it actually lands at Beauvais Airport (BVA)—which is located about 50 miles (80km) from Paris. You'll then have to pay an extra $20 to take a 1.5-hour bus ride to get into the city. Ryanair is notorious for this practice. However, this isn't always the case with every budget carrier so you'll have to do a little homework before booking.

Discount airlines are also very strict about check-in times so pay special attention to their policies. Don't expect any leeway. I once arrived at the check-in desk three minutes late and they refused to let me check-in. The flight wasn't schedule to depart for an hour but I was still turned away. My only option was to pay $100 for another ticket on the next plane.

While rare, some travelers will try to string together multiple flights to reach their destination. For example, you're trying to fly from Dublin to Budapest but there are no direct routes. So you book one flight from Dublin to Paris and then book another flight that leaves a few hours later from Paris to Budapest. However, if your first flight is late or delayed and you miss the next flight, the airline doesn't have any obligation to book you on a different one—even if you're flying the same airline. You're basically out of luck. Additionally, if you have checked luggage, you'll have to recheck it on the next flight.

BEST BOOKING WEBSITES

There are hundreds of airfare search engines—a few are excellent but most are mediocre at best. Here are my personal favorites so, between these recommended sites, you'll be able to find the best deal possible. Not only do these sites find the best prices, but they're also easy to use and have helpful extra features to assist in your search.

As you search, it's important to know that most super cheap tickets are often either nonrefundable or have steep ticket change fees—which may cost more than the original ticket.

SkyScanner.com is always my first stop when searching for tickets within Europe. It excels at finding a lot of the smaller European budget airlines that other sites sometimes miss. It also allows you to search by country and not just cities (for example, search for flights from Paris to Germany). This is a nice feature if you don't have a specific destination in mind.

Kayak.com is another trusty option that has always performed well. I use Kayak as a benchmark against other search engines.

Momondo.com, Hipmunk.com, and Dohop.com are three fairly new flight search engines but they all do an excellent job at finding both budget and normal flights throughout Europe. Momondo has some really cool analytic tools to help you choose the cheapest time to fly.

The airline's website. While most of the airfare search engines listed will find the best deals, it doesn't hurt to go directly to the airline's website. The three main budget carriers are Ryanair.com, easyJet.com, and airberlin.com. For example, Ryanair often has limited-time sales that search engines can't find.

Coach Travel

When one thinks of the ways to travel Europe, the bus (which is often called a "coach") is rarely on the top of the list. Yet, it is a popular choice for many budget travelers. The bus can be one of the most affordable methods of traveling though Europe, but it does lack the comfort, speed, and convenience of the train. Additionally, the schedules can often be fairly confusing and they get more complicated if you need to make transfers. However, in some countries—notably Ireland, Greece, Spain, Portugal, and a few Eastern European countries—the

rail network isn't extensive so the bus may be the best option.

Buses generally arrive/depart from bus stations but don't be surprised if it's just a parking lot. European bus stations can run the gamut from nice to kind of seedy—so that might be something to consider if you're arriving late at night since bus stations seem to attract "interesting" characters once the sun goes down. Bus stations are generally located toward the edge of towns.

Most major carriers operate modern bus fleets but the quality/cleanliness will differ by company. Many have reclining seats and restrooms, and Wi-Fi is becoming standard on the major companies. Buses drive on the same road as everyone else, so you're at the mercy of traffic. While not a huge problem on the motorways, traffic is often very bad in large cities. Be prepared for lots of stop-and-go driving and bring medicine if you easily get motion sickness.

Personally, I think the bus is only a good choice if flying or the train isn't a viable option. Bus journeys eat up a huge amount of time so you'll have to determine if the cost savings offset the extra time wasted on the road.

LONG-DISTANCE COACH COMPANIES

Eurolines is the largest and most popular bus company in Europe. They offer multiple routes to forty-plus cities throughout Europe and they're usually a pretty cheap way to travel. You can purchase point-to-point tickets, but they also offer travel passes (similar to rail passes) for fifteen or thirty days of unlimited travel. You'll get the best price on point-to-point tickets if you buy in advance.

Megabus is a low cost carrier within the United Kingdom. They offer service to most cities in the UK and they also have a few stops throughout Western Europe. It is fairly common to find $2 fares if you book early. I took a 4.5-hour Megabus journey from Leeds to London and I paid about $10 (and this was when the exchange rate was super high). I've found $4 tickets from London to Edinburgh (about a ten-hour journey) for tickets booked more than a month ahead—although ten hours on a bus might not be super comfortable. They're also starting to outfit their buses with free Wi-Fi.

National Express is Great Britain's largest bus network with more than one thousand destinations. Like Megabus, they also offer some super cheap seats to those who book early. They sell travel passes for unlimited travel within a set time period (7, 14, 28 days), but it might make more sense to just buy point-to-point tickets as needed.

iDBUS is a long-distance coach company owned by the French rail service that connects a few major cities in Europe (most in France or Italy).

Student Agency connects many Eastern/Northern Europe cities with Budapest and Prague.

Busabout is a "hop-on, hop-off" bus service for backpackers/younger travelers. They run a fleet of buses that follow predetermined circuits throughout Europe. A few different routes cater to specific parts of Europe (Western Europe, Southern Europe, Northern Europe, etc.). Each route has a number of designated cities where the bus stops. For example, the Northern Loop goes through Paris, Bruges, Amsterdam, Berlin, Dresden, Prague, Cesky Krumlov, Vienna, Salzburg, Munich, Stuttgart, and back to Paris (there might be an extra small town or two on that list). The nice thing is that you can stay in each city as long as you want and you can stay in whatever hostel/hotel you choose. Once you're ready to leave, you can simply hop on the next bus and be on your way to the next city.

Busabout does limit your travel a bit, but they do stop at a lot of the places you'd probably visit anyways (forty-one cities in total). Check Busabout.com for all their travel itineraries. This could be an option for someone who might be a little intimidated by European train/plane/bus travel. You're also going to be surrounded by other young travelers so that makes it easy to meet new friends.

Driving and Car Rentals

The best way to explore the countryside is by car.

If you want to get off the tourist trail and really explore Europe, then renting a car might be your perfect mode of transportation. Having a car allows you to visit all the tiny towns and villages that 99% of tourists never see. It gives you a chance to slow down and travel at your own pace. An American driver's license and passport is all that's needed to rent a car in Europe but

Europe is full of tiny streets and parking is scarce.

some countries (Austria, Greece, Hungary, Italy, Poland, Slovenia, and Spain) require an International Driving Permit (IDP)—which can be obtained via AAA.com before you arrive in Europe.

THINGS TO THINK ABOUT BEFORE RENTING A CAR

Your age. Many car companies require you to be twenty-one before they'll let you rent a car. Drivers under twenty-five will usually be charged an extra fee of around $30 per day

Busy cities. European cities are nightmares for drivers. Traffic is terrible, the streets are very confusing (European cities are not built on the "grid system"), and parking is very difficult and expensive. A car is great if you want to explore the countryside but might be more of a hassle if you plan on visiting only large cities.

Expensive gas and toll roads. Fuel is expensive in Europe. The cars are much more fuel-efficient, but fuel costs will still add up. In addition, there are many toll roads in Europe that can cost anywhere between $2.50 and $32.

Length of trip. It is more cost efficient to rent a car for a week or more because the cost per day goes down drastically the longer the rental period.

Extra fees. READ THE FINE PRINT. Car rental companies love to tack on all sorts of extra fees, so it is important to know all the exact costs when you make the reservation. Showing up at the car rental company to find that your rental is going to cost 30% to 50% more than you realized is never fun. Some examples of extra fees include:

- Dropping your car off in another country ($200–$300 extra)
- Dropping your car off at a different location
- Being under twenty-five
- Having more than one driver
- Tax (10%–30% on top of base price)
- Insurance ($15–$40/day)
- Automatic transmission ($100–$200/week)
- GPS unit
- Theft protection ($10–$30/day)
- City parking ($20–$50/day)
- Airport and train station drop-off fees

HOW TO RENT A CAR FOR THE BEST PRICE

I've found that AutoEurope.com and Europcar.com have the best prices, but it doesn't hurt to check the mega travel sites like Kayak, Skyscanner, Expedia, and Travelocity. Additionally, I also go directly to the major car rental company's websites like Hertz, Thrifty, Dollar, Budget, Avis, National, and Alamo to see if I can find a better deal. Like always, booking in advance is the best way to get the best deal.

One advantage to renting from a large company is that they have multiple locations. Booking from a large company might be smart if you plan on dropping your car off at a different location than where you picked it up. You'll most likely get charged a fee but the fee might be worth the hassle of getting back to your pick-up location.

Be aware that **many rental companies are closed on weekends and holidays** (Europeans have a lot of holidays). The booking website will usually alert you if the location is closed on your desired day but be sure to double-check.

Learn to drive a stick shift because automatic transmissions are not common in Europe. If you absolutely need an automatic, be sure to make reservations weeks in advance and be prepared to pay a hefty fee.

When you get the car, make sure to **note all existing damage**. Some shady companies will go over the car with a fine-toothed comb and charge you for damages they find—even if it was there when you picked it up.

BUY BACK CAR LEASE PROGRAM

If you plan on renting a car for a long period of time (between seventeen days and one year), it might be smart to lease a car. This method might seem a little unorthodox but you can save hundreds of dollars.

Like most strange things in Europe, the short-term lease program originated in France. You see, in France an extra 20% tax is added to the purchase price of new automobiles. However, non-European Union citizens are not subject to these extra taxes. Some wise guys thought, "hey, let's lease brand new cars to non-EU citizens and then have them 'sell' the car back to us after a few weeks. Then the car will technically be 'used' and not subject

to the 20% tax." Now there are multiple companies who do this buy back lease program and they sell them to businesses and car rental companies once the car is returned. Pretty clever.

BENEFITS TO SHORT-TERM LEASING

- You can save hundreds when compared to a traditional car rental.
- Like that new car smell? Your car comes straight from the factory.
- You get full comprehensive insurance (collision, fire, theft-of-vehicle, vandalism, and act-of-God) with zero deductible. The insurance is good in almost every European country.
- You only have to be 18 to lease a car.
- No extra taxes or surcharges.
- There are usually multiple pick-up/drop-off locations so you don't have to end your trip at the same location as you started.
- No fee for extra drivers.
- Unlimited mileage.
- Factory warranty and 24/7 roadside assistance.

DISADVANTAGES

- The car needs to be leased for at least seventeen to twenty-one days (depending on the auto company).

- These programs are usually based in France, so you normally have to pick up and drop off your car in France. Most companies allow you to drop the car off outside France for an additional charge, but you don't have as many location options compared to a large rental-car company.

SHORT-TERM LEASE COMPANIES

There are a handful of reputable companies who offer the buy back program and they all operate similarly—IdeaMerge (ideamerge.com/motoeuropa), Europe by Car (europebycarblog.com), Renault USA (renaultusa.com), AutoEurope Peugeot Program (autoeurope.com/buyback_home.cfm).

Rideshares and Hitchhiking

If you're on an extreme budget and want to make your parents worried sick, then you might want to consider hopping in a car with a stranger. Your two best options are good ol' hitchhiking or an organized rideshare. I'm not going to lecture you on the potential dangers of these two options but use your best judgment, and, if possible, travel with someone else.

Hitchhiking can be hit or miss in terms of success. In Germany, for example, hitchhiking is popular and you can probably get a ride without much effort. On the other hand, hitchhikers in Italy and Spain complain about having to wait a few hours before anyone will give them a ride. It's always important to have a backup plan in case you can't find a ride. A great resource for hitchhiking is Hitchwiki (hitchwiki.org/en/europe). It covers everything you need to know about this form of transportation, so I highly suggest reading through the entire site.

Ridesharing is another option for traveling across Europe inexpensively. It does take a little bit of searching to find people taking the same route as you, but it is usually simple to find a ride—especially if you're traveling between popular destinations. The good thing about rideshares is the added predictability since the trip is prearranged with the driver. However, you will have to pay for the ride. Do look into bus travel if you're considering this option, as the bus fare could be similarly priced.

The most popular ridesharing site is the German website Mitfahrgelegenheit—which translates to "drive-with-opportunity" (mitfahrgelegenheit.de). A lot of the listings are in German but it's still pretty easy to navigate. Bla Bla Car (blablacar.com) is another great ridesharing site and it is in English. Other less popular websites are hitchhikers.org, myrideboard.eu, and carpooling.co.uk.

CHAPTER FIVE— TRAVEL SAFETY AND AVOIDING TOURIST SCAMS

When it comes to safety in Europe, the main thing you need to worry about is petty crime—specifically pickpockets and less frequently robbery. Violent crime is rare and gun-related crime is virtually nonexistent. Of course, there are a few cities that have elevated crime rates and you should always use commonsense safety precautions, but the chances of anything happening is extremely low.

Pickpockets and Petty Theft

If you're planning a trip to Europe, you've undoubtedly been warned about the danger of pickpockets. It is important to be vigilant because thousands of tourists are victims of pickpockets each year—and no one wants to spend their hard-earned vacation trying to cancel their credit cards, replacing their passport, and finding alternative means to access money. Luckily there are many simple things you can do to deter yourself from becoming a pickpocketing victim.

POPULAR CITIES FOR PICKPOCKETS

While pickpockets can be found in nearly any city, but the largest concentrations are in cities that attract the most tourists (no surprise there). Below is a list of pickpocket hotspots in Europe:

- Barcelona, Spain
- Rome, Italy
- Paris, France
- Madrid, Spain
- Athens, Greece
- Prague, Czech Republic
- Lisbon, Portugal
- Florence, Italy
- London, England
- Amsterdam, Netherlands

But don't think that pickpocketing only occurs in big cities. I have a friend who had his wallet stolen in a small town in Switzerland, so it's wise to keep your guard up.

WHO ARE THE PICKPOCKETS?

This group of pickpockets got caught— most don't.

Most people assume pickpockets are sketchy looking men, but a large number of pickpockets are actually young girls and boys—usually around ten to sixteen years old. Most tourists don't suspect a young child would steal from them so they let their guard down. Additionally, police have a harder time arresting minors and most travel without any sort of identification, so even if they're caught, the police usually have to let them go. Other times pickpockets are well dressed and you'd never expect them to be thieves.

Pickpockets almost always work in groups. One or two people will do something to distract the victim while another member tries to take their stuff. Once the theft has occurred, the thief who stole the item will often hand it off to someone else and they'll all run in separate directions. This makes it very hard to track the culprit.

PICKPOCKET HOT SPOTS

Tourists attractions. Whether it's the Eiffel Tower in Paris, the Trevi Fountain in Rome, or the Charles Bridge in Prague, it isn't a surprise that pickpockets hang out in busy tourist spots. Naturally, tourists are more concerned about viewing the sights and taking photos than being attentive to their surroundings.

Pickpockets love big crowds.

Public transportation. Subways and city buses are prime spots for pickpockets—and after living in Paris, I've seen my fair share of pickpockets on the Paris Metro. Public transportation is a great place for a pickpocket because it is often very crowded and it is easy for thieves to create confusion. Pickpockets normally target large metro/subway stations where many transit lines converge because it gives them plenty of places to exit if they're being chased by the police.

Museums. During the summer, Europe's most popular museums swell to maximum capacity and there are bound to be a few pickpockets among the lot. While the admission price deters most pickpockets, it doesn't stop all of them from preying on unsuspecting visitors who are simply enjoying the art. In fact, in 2013 the workers at the Louvre Museum in Paris went on strike because the pickpockets were getting so bad.

Train stations. Trains stations are large, crowded, and full of confused tourists with their hands full of cumbersome luggage—which is exactly the kind of environment pickpockets love.

Restaurants, cafes, and bars. Many people let their guard down when they're enjoying a meal or a drink, so it is easy for a crook to sneakily snatch a purse from the back of a chair or a mobile phone from the top of a table.

The beach. Pay attention to your stuff when you're at the beach. Don't leave your bag unattended or out of sight because there is a good chance someone might snatch them. And no, hiding things in your shoes isn't fooling anyone.

Retail stores. Clothing and departments stores in Europe can get extremely crowded—especially around the holidays. It is an easy place for a pickpocket to target tourists that are usually carrying a lot of money.

TRICKS PICKPOCKETS USE

Distraction is the one tactic that all pickpockets use. They want to distract your attention just long enough to take your stuff. The following methods are well-known ways that pickpockets and thieves steal from tourists.

"Charity" worker with clipboards. This scam is very popular in Paris. It nearly always involves a group of young girls with clipboards. They'll approach you and point to a clipboard while motioning that they're deaf and mute. They want you to sign a petition for charity. If you sign, they'll ask for a donation to the charity. Of course the "charity" is fake—in fact, frequently the money often goes to these girls' "boss" (i.e., human traffickers). While the tourist is signing/reading the petition, there is often an accomplice trying to pickpocket the victim.

Crowd the subway. Subway trains can get very crowded. A common tactic is for a group of four to six children to push onto a packed train shortly before the doors shut and crowd their target. They'll swipe what they're trying to steal and then they all hop off right before the doors begin to close. By the time the victim realizes what happened, it is too late and the train has already left the station.

Always be wary when a group of people crowd onto an already busy metro car. Also be suspicious of anyone who is standing very close to you on a train that isn't crowded because they might be up to no good.

Smartphone grab. Thieves love smartphones because they're valuable and easy to steal. That's why it's generally advisable to avoid using your smartphone while you're on public transportation. However, if you do, ensure that you sit away from the doors. It is common for thieves to reach in and snatch the victim's phone right before the doors close.

Help with your bag. Some subway stations have numerous stairs so "good Samaritans" will forcibly grab your suitcase to help you carry it up the stairs. This usually takes the victim off-guard and that is when their accomplice reaches into your purse or pocket.

However, there are actually a lot of nice people who will offer to help carry your heavy suitcase if they see you struggling. The main difference between them and the bad guys is that they'll ask you before grabbing your bag.

Bump and lift. When you're surrounded by crowds, it isn't uncommon to accidentally bump into other people. However, this is a classic move performed by pickpockets, so if someone bumps into you, it might be smart to take a quick inventory of your belongings.

Escalator backup. Escalators are another area that pickpockets target because it is easy to create chaos. With this scam, there will be one or two people in front of the target and a few behind the target. Someone near the top of the escalator will stop right when they get off and this will create a huge backup for people trying to get off. As the backup occurs, the people behind the target will reach into the target's bag/pocket and hand off the goods to one of his buddies behind him. I've also seen where they've handed off the goods to someone on the opposite escalator so it's almost impossible to chase them.

Newspaper/map distraction. A common pickpocket tactic involves using a large map or a newspaper to cover the target's line of sight to take things out of his or her bag. They'll shove the map in your face, point to a part of the map, and then their accomplice will reach under the paper so you can't see what they're taking. This is a very common way people steal mobile phones from tables.

ATM confusion. Always be careful when using the ATM—especially when you're alone. While you're in the process of withdrawing money, a group of beggars will approach you from behind to try and get your attention. They might pull on your arm or shove a piece of paper in front of the screen. If you turn toward one of the thieves, another one will slip in from the other side and press the button for the max amount of cash. Then they'll swipe the money and run off. If this happens, put your hand where the money is being dispensed because that is where the thieves will be targeting.

Also be sure to cover up your pin code when you enter it. Some thieves will try to see your code (some even use hidden cameras) and then they'll follow you around for a chance to steal your card.

The helpful tourist. Don't let pickpockets take advantage of your good nature. In this scam, one of the scammers will drop something in front of you and while you're helping them pick up the mess, the other pickpocket will swoop in and lift something from you bag. That doesn't mean you can't help your fellow man but be mindful about your own stuff while helping.

Slashed bag. Some pickpockets don't even bother trying to open your bag and they will simply slash it open with a knife. This is fairly uncommon in Europe but it isn't unheard of.

Turnstile stall. Busy turnstiles are a common area for pickpockets to strike. As you're approaching a turnstile, one person will cut in front of you and then proceed to stop (they might pretend that the machine isn't working) and their partner will come up behind you—essentially trapping you between the two of them. The person in the back will lift something from your bag or pocket while his partner in the front is fumbling with the turnstile.

Scooter snatch and run. While not super common, some thieves will drive up on a scooter, snatch a bag from the victim's shoulder, and then ride off into the sunset. I wouldn't be too worried about this technique but it can happen.

Street performances. In popular tourists spots there are multiple street performers who'll dance, play music, or put on some type of performance. They can draw quite a crowd, but beware because it's a popular area for pickpockets to target.

Fake fight. A large group of men will pretend to start an altercation around a target, and in all the commotion one of the men will attempt to pickpocket the target.

Enjoy the show but watch your wallet.

WHO PICKPOCKETS TARGET

Anyone can be a potential target of a pickpocket, but they do tend to target certain types of people. Pickpockets will always look for the easiest target because they don't want a confrontation.

Tourist. Tourist = money in the mind of a pickpocket. If you look like a tourist, you're automatically going to be singled out. This is one of the benefits of dressing like a local.

People with a lot of luggage. If you are pulling along two suitcases and have a backpack, you're going to be a prime target for a pickpocket. You won't be able to watch over all your things too closely since you have so much stuff.

Asians. Asians (specifically the Chinese) are a top choice for pickpockts because many of the Chinese who travel to Europe are very wealthy. Additionally, a large number of Chinese citizens don't have easy access to credit and debit cards, so they often travel with large amounts of cash—and thieves know this. So even if you're not Chinese but have Asian heritage, you might want to be more cautions.

People who flash valuables. Walking alone at night while using your iPhone? Don't be surprised if someone takes it away from you.

Trusting people. From all my travels, I've rarely met a friendlier bunch than the Australians. I've also rarely met another group of people who've been victims of pickpockets more than the Australians. I think the people who think everyone else around them is nice and helpful are the ones who get taken advantage of most often.

HOW TO PROTECT YOUR-SELF FROM PICKPOCKETS

If you've made it this far, you might be thinking that there are thousands of pickpockets trying to rob every tourist in Europe. But that isn't the case and you'll rarely have any problems if you take a few extra precautions. It is also important to remember that actual violent crime is really quite low in Europe, so as long as you're vigilant, you'll be safe. In this section, we'll talk about what steps to take to avoid becoming a victim.

Limit what you carry. Pickpockets can't steal what you don't have —simple. That is why I prefer to carry very little while I'm sightseeing. I especially recommend not carrying a lot of cash.

Wear a money belt. Personally, I hate money belts, but it is one of the most secure ways to carry valuables like extra money and your passport. However, many tourists make the mistake of thinking that they should use their money belt like a wallet—it isn't intended for that. Ideally, you should keep the money and debit/credit cards that you're going to need for the day in your wallet and then keep all extra cash and maybe a backup credit card in the money belt. The money belt should be worn under your clothes and should be fairly inconvenient to access (to deter thieves).

Keep wallet in front pocket. A lot of guys keep their wallets in their back pockets, but this is an extremely easy target for a pickpocket. This is why it is advisable to keep your wallet in your front pocket. I highly recommend getting a super thin wallet because a bulky wallet feels very strange in your front pocket—and it looks kind of dumb.

Keep phones off the table. Smartphones are a super popular item for thieves to target. Many people will simply leave it on the table while they're eating and someone can easily come up and snatch it.

Split up your valuables. Don't keep all your eggs in one basket. Split up your valuables so if you are pickpocketed you'll limit the amount you've lost.

Lock it up. Hostels are safe and I've never had any problems with theft, but it is still smart to lock any valuables in a locker.

Secure your bag/backpack. Your bag or backpack is probably the most vulnerable area that pickpockets love to target. Backpacks are especially vulnerable because you can't see if someone is trying to get into it. Here are some tips for securing your bag:

- **Wear it backwards**. When you're on crowded public transportation, a lot of people will wear their bags backwards because it's easier to keep an eye on it.
- **Lock the zippers**. At a minimum, you'll want to lock your zippers. You don't need anything fancy—a simple luggage lock will work well.
- **Sling backpack.** Sling backpacks are nice because they stay close to your body and

they can be slung over your chest easily if needed. They do tend to be small, so you'll have trouble if you plan on carrying a lot of stuff with you.

- **Secure bag to an immovable object.** When you're at a restaurant, loop your bag's strap around your leg or the leg of your chair so someone can't come by and swipe the bag. Similarly, it is smart to secure your bag to a chair or luggage rack while you're on a train—especially on overnight trains. A retractable cable lock will provide enough protection to deter most thieves.

- **Pickpocket proof bags.** If you want to be extra safe, you can get yourself a specially designed "pickpocket proof" backpack, bag, or purse. A company called Pacsafe makes the most popular antitheft bags. Their bags have tamperproof zippers, cut-proof straps, anchored straps, and a slash-proof metal mesh sewn into the bag. However, their bags are fairly expensive and all that extra protection could be a little overkill—but the added peace of mind is worth the extra price for some people.

ATM/Credit Card/Debit Card Fraud

Credit card fraud is a multi-billion dollar industry and scammers frequently target tourists. In Europe, thieves are getting clever when it comes to this type of fraud. Here are some ways to help protect yourself.

Credit/debit card skimming. It is EXTREMELY easy to "clone" (aka skim) a credit card. In fact, skimming is one of the biggest problems in bank fraud today because anyone can buy a skimmer online for a few hundred dollars. The thief simply needs to swipe your card though a tiny card reader that records all the info from the card's magnetic strip. Most often it is waiters and shopkeepers that commit this crime since they're the people who are handling your bankcards. Sometimes they'll make charges right away, but they'll often wait months before they make a charge.

Always use your credit card (or cash) when making purchases at a place of business. It is much easier to contest fraudulent charges with a credit card. It can be a huge nightmare if your debit card gets cloned because it takes much longer to get your money back.

I've had my cards cloned—twice. They didn't make any purchases until about three months after my trip. One day I randomly had a charge from Spain for $1,800 and I hadn't even visited Spain during my trip. Luckily, my credit card company declined it before it went through.

Never use your credit card on a payphone. Many payphones will give you the option to use your credit card to make a call and then you'll get charged an insane amount. I know someone who paid well over $50 for a two-minute call. This isn't technically illegal but it is still a scam.

Cash machines. The ATM is another place you need to be wary about getting scammed. Always hide your PIN from prying eyes. Thieves have been known to rig up small cameras pointed to the number pad so always use your other hand to hide your code.

Another common scam is to put clear tape in the card slot, which results in your card getting stuck when it is inserted. After you leave, someone comes by with tweezers and retrieves your card. Go inside the bank if your card gets stuck and cancel it if they can't retrieve it.

While fairly rare, some thieves outfit ATMs with a cloning device (like mentioned earlier) and steal hundreds of credit numbers. This is a pretty advanced technique and it can be difficult to detect. If the ATM looks a little funny, I suggest finding another one.

Crooked Taxis

Ahh yes. The dreaded taxi. It feels like even the honest ones are trying to rip you off. Unfortunately, there are plenty of drivers who set out to scam unsuspecting tourists—especially in Eastern Europe. Here are some of the common scams to look out for when taking taxis.

Use official taxis. All legitimate taxis have to follow certain rules and regulations. However, there are plenty of unlicensed, illegal, and private car services that don't follow the same guidelines. Official taxis will have some type of accreditation posted in the taxi.

Use taxi stands. Taxi stands are places where legitimate taxis line up to pick up passengers. Unfortunately, you can't assume they'll all be honest but it is your best bet.

Call for a taxi. If you can't find a taxi that seems legitimate, you can call a well-known taxi company and they'll come pick you up.

Go by the meter. Many crooked drivers will claim the meter is "broken" or they won't turn it on because of some other excuse. They're always going to rip you off in these cases. Insist that they turn it on. Leave if they don't.

Only use clearly marked official taxis.

Know normal prices. Remember that knowledge is power. Seek out an unbiased third party (hostel, Internet, friend, etc.) to give you a close guess to how much you should be paying for your ride. Another tip is to ask the cab driver for this estimated cost before you get in and compare the two.

Bags in the backseat. While rare, some cabs have been known to keep your bags as ransom until you pay their inflated fees.

Carry small bills. Some drivers might claim not to have small change so you get back less money than you should.

Clearly count your money. Hand your money to the driver slowly, bill by bill. Then make sure you get all your change back. And double-check again.

Never take recommendations. Always be wary about taxi drivers who lure you to an establishment they recommend—they may just be doing it to receive a commission.

Flirty Women And Strip Club Scams

Friendly local females. A *super* common scam involves a pretty girl (or two) and alcohol. They'll approach you on the street and start flirting with you. And since we males are dumb, we actually believe the pretty ladies are genuinely interested in us. They'll eventually invite you a bar/club/restaurant that they know. At the bar, they'll ask that you buy them a drink. What you don't know is that the girls and the bar are scamming you. Each drink costs a few hundred dollars (they don't tell you this) and at the end of the night you're stuck with a $1000-plus bill.

When the bill arrives, the girls are magically nowhere to be found but the lovely ladies have been replaced by a few scary dudes who want "their" money. They'll happily escort you to the nearest ATM while you withdraw your cash. This scam is *very* widespread in Eastern Europe but it happens everywhere. Many times the police won't do anything about it so you're out of luck.

Strip clubs. I advise against going to strip clubs because tourists are scammed there *all* the time. Much like the scam above, you'll be charged exorbitant amounts for drinks/talking to the hostess/whatever else you do at a strip club. It's not unheard of for the bouncers to hold you at knifepoint until you fork over a few hundred dollars.

Money Scams

Menus change. Some scummy restaurants will have two menus—one with normal prices and then another higher price. They'll show you the normal price when you order and then they'll give you a large bill. When you protest, they'll show you the menu with the high prices.

Menu without prices. I wouldn't eat at a restaurant that doesn't advertise its prices. You're just asking to get ripped off if you do.

Fake undercover police. A common scam involves "undercover" police wanting to check your money because they think you have counterfeit bills. They'll inspect your money and trade it out for small bills without you noticing. They'll often flash a badge to make it all look official. Plainclothes officers don't deal with tourists, so ask them to bring a police car before you'll give them any access to your cash.

Street moneychangers. Never change money in the street. It is usually illegal and you're going to get ripped off. If you need to change money, go to an official change office.

Short change. Shop keepers, taxi drivers, and other lovely people will probably try to shortchange you at least once during your trip. It is the worst in countries that don't use the euro because the money is so foreign to tourists. Make sure you count all your money carefully before leaving the register.

Computer Scams

Accessing the Internet is virtually a necessity for the modern traveler but you should be aware of the potential dangers you might come across—especially when using public computers or Wi-Fi.

It's important to understand that you're always potentially at risk when you use Wi-Fi because whoever controls the wireless router can technically intercept the data that's transmitted over their network. Therefore you should always think twice before entering passwords, credit card info, or doing online banking. The only real way to ensure your information is safe is by using a cellular data plan.

You should also be cautious when using public computers at hostels or Internet cafés. Many of these computers have nasty viruses and key loggers that are designed to steal your information. It's advisable to use Google Chrome or Firefox because they have extra built-in security features. Both browsers have portable versions that can be run off a USB key—which adds a little extra security.

Other Tourist Scams

Here are a few other scams and safety issues you should know about.

Mugging. Violent crime is rare but there are still plenty of cases of muggings. It's common sense but not making yourself an easy target should deter most muggings. Don't wear flashy jewelry and be smart about using your smartphone at night. Stick to busy, well-lit streets at night. Also be extra cautious when using the ATM alone—night or day. If you can, use an ATM that is inside and not on the street.

And finally, walk with confidence. Muggers generally want to attack the weak so you should always act like you know exactly where you are and that you belong there.

Drug and alcohol safety. When most travelers, especially young travelers, get in trouble, it is usually accompanied by alcohol. So be smart about your drinking. Just like at home, don't accept drinks from random people and don't leave your drink alone.

Ticket machines dupe. Always be a little leery of people who try to help you at ticket machines. I know some people who got scammed in Paris from a well-dressed man who "helped" them buy metro tickets. They wanted to buy two five-day passes, which costs about $50 each, so the man offered to use his credit card because he told them Australian bankcards don't work in the machines. He said that they could just pay him in cash. He did buy them tickets, but he bought them a one-way child's ticket (which looks very similar to a five-day pass) that cost about $1.50 and he pocketed the $100.

General Safety Tips

There are a lot of little things that can be potentially dangerous that we sometimes forget about when we're traveling. Pay attention to traffic. Every year, a handful of tourists are killed in London because they forget that traffic comes from the opposite direction. Be careful when walking under scaffolding because construction workers sometimes drop things. I once had a large bucket full of concrete powder fall about two feet in front of me. It fell from the seventh floor and it probably weighed at least 50lbs. That would have been a bad day if it had landed on my head. Pay attention to trams because they're very quiet and the tracks blend into the road so they can be hard to see.

CHAPTER SIX—
SOLO AND GROUP
TRAVEL

Your travel partners can either enhance or completely ruin your travels. You'll encounter stressful situations, so it's important to know how the group dynamic will function in these situations. Or maybe you want to head out on your own and rely on yourself. Whatever you choose, it's important to know what you're getting yourself into so you can ensure a successful time abroad.

Solo Travel Advice

My first backpacking trip in Europe was a solo adventure. I was a little worried at first (as were my parents), but I was surprised how many other solo travelers I met along the way. It took me a day or two to adjust to traveling alone, but I quickly realized how rewarding solo travel could be. This section will cover the positives and the negatives of traveling Europe alone and give you some practical advice on how to make the most of your travels.

POSITIVE ASPECTS OF SOLO TRAVEL

Choose your own itinerary. When you travel alone, you have the freedom to do the things you want to do

and you don't need to answer to anyone else. In a group, everyone has their own ideas of what to see and this can cause a lot of conflict.

Food freedom. From my experience, choosing where to eat can cause more stress than just about anything else—especially when you're traveling with a group of people. When you travel alone, you can choose exactly where to eat. Also, many restaurants in Europe won't split up the bill, so paying becomes a huge hassle in large groups.

No arguments. Travel can be stressful and you usually take out your frustration on your travel partners—it's inevitable. Even best friends have been known to get into huge fights after a few weeks of constant travel. However, when you're on your own, you have no one to argue with.

Total focus. There is no one to "distract" you so you're totally focused on whatever it is you're experiencing.

Reinvent yourself. You can be whoever you want to be when you travel alone. This is your chance to let loose.

Meet new people. I meet a lot more people when I travel alone. Groups tend, usually unknowingly, to put up a "wall" between themselves and other travelers, so this makes groups not as approachable. You also have an instant connection with other solo travelers.

Self-growth. You have no one but yourself to rely on when you're a solo traveler. It might be a struggle at first but you quickly learn to be self-reliant—and I think that makes you a stronger person.

DISADVANTAGES OF SOLO TRAVEL

Eating alone. A lot of people feel really uncomfortable eating alone—especially in restaurants. It isn't bad for breakfast and lunch, but dinners do get a little lonely. It really isn't that bad and it isn't too hard to find other people to eat with, but it can be a little unnerving.

Unwanted isolation. Staying in hostels is great because there are almost always tons of other people around to hang out with, but there will be times where you'll find yourself alone.

I remember my very first night of solo traveling. I was in Dublin and the hostel was overrun by a large group of Spanish students. There must have been about forty of them. I didn't meet any English speakers that first night so it was pretty lonely. I was also a new traveler so I was quite timid. Luckily, occasions like this were rare, and I became more outgoing the more I traveled.

No "buddy system." It can be nice to have a buddy to share your memories with and to help keep each other safe.

HOW TO SUCCESSFULLY TRAVEL SOLO

Stay in hostels. There are plenty of ways to meet other people while you're traveling solo. The easiest is at your hostel. There will nearly always be someone looking to meet up. This is also a great opportunity to meet with other solo travelers.

Be friendly and outgoing. Smile and be the first person to introduce yourself. If someone new arrives at the hostel, greet him or her. I didn't do a very good job being outgoing my first few nights, so I had a hard time meeting people. But after the third night, I forced myself to be a little more outgoing and it opened up so many doors.

Beer. Buy some cheap beer and offer it to people. You'll meet TONS of people this way. People will often do the same for you.

Cook meals in the hostel. You'll meet so many people if you hang out in the kitchen around dinnertime. This is also a good time to hand out those beers.

Hostel planned activities. Many hostels plan outings like free walking tours or pub-crawls. This is an easy way to meet other travelers.

Seek out other people. Most big cities have an active Couchsurfing meet-up community that gets together each week. It's normally held at a bar and anyone is welcome. It's a great place to meet other travelers, expats, and locals. Additionally, most major cities have free walking tours that attract a lot of younger travelers.

Start in a country where you know the language. Traveling is confusing—especially when you're solo. Traveling in a country where you don't know the language is even more confusing. That is why I recommend starting out in the UK or Ireland because you can always ask someone if you have a question. If nothing else, it lets you ease into international travel a bit easier, and it will help build your travel acumen.

Plan ahead to avoid confusion. It is wise to have your accommodation arranged before you arrive in each city. This way you'll know exactly where to go the second you step off the train or plane. I also recommend spending a little time studying how to get to your hostel before you arrive. If you're familiar with how the public transportation works or what route to walk, you'll remove much of the stress of traveling. Additionally, planning ahead keeps you from wandering around aimlessly—which thieves pick up on very quickly.

Take it easy on yourself and relax. Traveling is stressful. You'll make mistakes. Things will go wrong. You'll feel defeated at some point. It is natural, and all travelers go through it. I hit a wall after about three weeks of traveling, but I powered through it and I felt better after having a few bad days.

I recommend doing something nice for yourself or doing something "normal." Go see a movie. Have a bit of retail therapy. Sign up for a cooking class or a wine tasting. It will help rejuvenate you.

Take a guided tour the first day. Guided tours are a great way to become familiar with a city. If you're feeling overwhelmed, take one of those hop-on/hop-off bus tours because it gives you a good idea how the city is laid out. Then when I'm exploring the city by foot, I have a little better idea of where I am in relation to the other sights. Another great option is a bike tour or a walking tour.

Ask people to take your picture. I have a thousand photos of Europe, but I'm only in about a dozen of them. I didn't even realize it until I got back home and started looking through my pictures—I still regret not having more. People are more than willing to take your photo, but you just have to ask.

Pack light. The more stuff you drag along with you, the more difficult traveling becomes—especially when you're traveling alone.

Safety first. Use your common sense. It probably isn't the best idea to walk around large cities at night by yourself. Actually, I've done this many times and never felt unsafe. Just be sure to stay alert. If something doesn't feel right, then you shouldn't do it. Always walk with confidence and act like you've done so a million times.

Write down the address of your accommodation. Always have the name and address of where you're staying. This is important because it is easy to get lost in many European cities—their streets don't use the grid system, so finding your way home can be difficult. Plus, good luck trying to tell your taxi driver to take you to 27 Scheepstimmermanstraat (yes, this is a real street name).

Arrive to new locations during the day. Whether it's at a train station or an airport, one of the most confusing and frustrating moments of traveling is when you first arrive in a new city. But things get much more difficult when you arrive at night because help desks are often closed, other travelers are gone, and people seem a little sketchier. That is why I try my best to arrive during the day.

I once arrived in Bruges late at night and I had no idea where my hostel was located. Normally, I would get a map from the tourist booth but they were closed. I wandered around for a solid hour before I found it and

the door was locked. That's when I learned that not all hostels have 24/7 reception.

That night I found out how much sleeping on a bench in a train station sucks. If I had arrived in the day, I would have found the hostel in about 15 minutes and could have spent the night enjoying a great Belgian beer.

Choose accommodation in popular areas. I always feel safer when my hostel is located in a fairly popular part of town. I'd much rather be walking around alone in a busy neighborhood than a deserted one. This is something to watch out for when booking accommodations because some of the cheaper options are in less desirable locations.

Know your neighborhood. Before you head out for the day, take a look at a map to get familiar with your route, the areas you're visiting, and the neighborhood you're staying in.

Guide to Solo Travel for Women

Women shouldn't be afraid of traveling alone. In fact, I met just as many solo female travelers as I did solo male travelers. However, it's smart for females to take a few extra precautions. In this section, we'll cover some basic safety tips and advice for ensuring a successful solo journey through Europe.

SAFETY ADVICE FOR SOLO WOMEN TRAVELERS

The main reason most females don't travel alone usually boils down to safety concerns. It is smart to be vigilant when you're traveling alone, but you shouldn't feel unsafe about traveling by yourself. I know I felt safer walking the streets in Europe than I do in the United States. The advice in this section is common sense, but it is a good idea to read through it so it's fresh in your mind.

Be aware. The best safety advice I could give a solo traveler, or any traveler for that matter, is to simply be aware of your surroundings. That doesn't mean you have to be paranoid about everything, but it is important to have an idea of what is going around you.

Protect your bag or purse. One of the biggest threats is getting your purse or bag snatched. I suggest keeping your bag in your lap when seated at a restaurant. If you have a larger bag that is uncomfortable to keep in your lap, then make sure to loop the shoulder strap around the leg of your chair so someone can't run by and snatch it.

Find a group when going out at night. It might not be fair but women need to be more vigilant when they're out at night. Remember: safety in numbers.

Act like you belong. Predators pick up on fear and confusion and that is why you need to always act like you belong. Act like you know exactly where you are going. Exude confidence! Walk with purpose—even if you are lost. As a female traveling alone, this is an important thing to remember.

Listen to your gut. When you're traveling alone, it is important to listen to your instincts. If something doesn't feel right, then it probably isn't. It's cliché advice but it is important.

Avoid dangerous situations with alcohol. We've all done some dumb things while drinking, but we're usually around friends. I don't have to tell you that getting really drunk in an unfamiliar city with a bunch of people you don't know very well isn't the best idea.

Don't flash valuables. It is always smart to be careful about not flashing money and valuables around for people to see. Leave fancy jewelry at home, try to not use your phone alone on the street (especially at night or on public transportation), and if something feels wrong you should try to hop into a store or get close to a group of people.

Be careful when using the ATM. As a solo traveler, one of your most vulnerable moments will be when you're withdrawing money from an ATM because you don't have anyone to watch your back. I suggest withdrawing money inside the bank and not on the street.

Female-only dorms (optional). Most hostel rooms are mixed gender, but many offer a few female-only rooms. Most women feel completely safe in hostel dorms because there is always a pretty equal mix of both sexes. But if you feel safer in a female-only dorm, choose that option.

Getting hit on by men in public. You're going to get hit on by men— more so in some countries than others. It is inevitable. It is usually pretty harmless but some guys can take it too far. If you don't want to deal with it, there are a few precautions you can take to ward off those unwanted advances.

The most common piece of advice is to wear a fake wedding band because this will deter most advances by would-be Rico Suaves.

In many countries, eye contact is taken as a sign of flirting. Even an accidental glance gives many guys the impression that you want to chat. The easiest way to avoid these situations is by wearing sunglasses . . . but you're on your own when you're inside or at night.

If some guy starts talking to you (and you're not interested in talking to him), then you should simply ignore him. If you respond, don't be surprised if he continues trying to chat you up. A lot of women suggest wearing a pair of earbuds while on public transportation, as it is a clear sign that you don't want to chat.

Join a tour. If you're still uneasy about traveling Europe alone, but don't have a travel partner, you can use a tour company like Contiki Tours, Busabout, and a few others that are catered directly to younger travelers.

Tips for Traveling with Friends and Significant Others

Keep the head-butts to a minimum.

Backpacking in Europe with your friends can create amazing lifelong memories—or it can be a complete disaster. Travel is often stressful, especially when you're in a foreign environment, and we tend to take out our frustration on the people we're traveling with. There are numerous stories about best friends ceasing to talk to each other for months after the trip had ended—this is way more common than you think. I'm sure just as many relationships have ended because of traveling abroad. While you won't be able to remove all the stress, you can take some steps to help lower the likelihood of getting into major fights. This section will give you some tips that could save your vacation and friendship and/or relationship.

PRE-TRIP CONSIDER-ATIONS

Small groups work best. If you're going to travel with friends, it's best to keep your group small. Anything over four people is asking for trouble. Everyone has their own ideas and opinions, and the chance for conflict grows as the group grows. It becomes very difficult to satisfy everyone's expectations so everyone's enjoyment suffers in the end.

Communicate and compare travel styles. A huge source of conflict arises when travel partners don't know each other's travel style. Sit down and see what each person expects before traveling. Chart out a rough destination itinerary that all parties can agree on. Naturally, there will be compromise, but if there is already tension at this stage, then there might be cause for concern.

First consider each person's budget expectation because money can be a source of conflict. One member of the group might be an extreme penny-pincher and may never want to spend money on anything—no museums, no attractions, only takes the cheapest transportation, eats cheese and bread for every meal, etc. This person could drag the group down with their unwillingness to spend any money. Alternatively, you could be on a tight budget while the other members in your group have plenty of cash, so you end up spending way more than you anticipated.

Next, determine the types of activities each person would like to do while traveling. Someone who wants to go shopping all the time could butt heads with partners who want to spend all day in museums.

Travel pace is another important factor. You may be more interested in soaking up the culture and ambiance whereas your partner would rather see as much as possible. Both styles are perfectly good choices but it has potential to cause tension.

Another thing that people forget about is finding out if your travel partners are morning people. You may want to be out the door by 8 a.m. but your partner would rather sleep in a bit more. It's all about coming to an agreement so everyone is on the same page.

Finally, it's important to remember that your travel partner's personality will be amplified after you've spent so much time together. If they're overbearing, uptight, negative, unadventurous, worrisome, etc., you will want to take that into consideration.

DURING THE TRIP ADVICE

Schedule alone time. Don't forget that you don't have to do everything together. This is huge and *every* experienced group-traveler will tell you this. Let the group split up and have everyone do his or her own thing. This will help keep everyone sane and hopefully out of jail. I recommend actually planning alone time into your schedule from the very start. Don't wait for emotions to boil over because the alone time will be painted in a negative light.

Everyone pay separate. I prefer that everyone pays for their own stuff during the trip. Some people suggest having everyone put in a small amount of cash if you're going to cook a meal. Settle any "debts" the same day.

Communication. Everyone should speak up and give their input about what the group does. Don't bottle it all up and get frustrated because people can't read your mind.

Be on time. Your time is limited, so it is important to stick to the agreed times. The biggest problems usually arise during the morning because many people have trouble getting up on time. Also, being on time is especially important when you have to catch a train/plane.

Figure out the food. One of the biggest causes of tension while traveling is food. There never seems to be a restaurant around when you start to get hungry. This causes the group to wander around while trying to find something to eat that everyone can agree on. And when people are hungry, they get grumpy. Write down a handful of restaurants (or grocery stores) in the area of the city you'll be exploring. If you have this list ready to go, you'll prevent a lot of stress.

Be flexible and compromise. Things are going to go wrong and you can't always get your way—but you have to deal with it.

Chill out. Travel is stressful and every group will have conflict. It is important to remember to step back and relax. Don't take out your frustrations on the people you're traveling with. It is very easy to get so caught up in the "fight" that you forget you're visiting some of the most amazing cities in the world. Don't forget to apologize when you lose your cool.

CHAPTER SEVEN—
DAY-TO-DAY
MONEY-SAVING
STRATEGIES

There is nothing better than having a picnic in a park.

Cheap travel can be difficult in Europe, and many travelers end up spending a lot more money than they need to—especially on day-to-day things—simply because they're unaware of money-saving strategies. I've compiled a list of simple money-saving tips to help stretch your travel dollars.

Eat, Drink, and Be Merry

As a budget traveler, you have to get a little creative when it comes to eating and drinking or you will quickly blow through your travel fund. Luckily, there are plenty of options for the cash-strapped backpacker, and they don't involve eating solely ramen noodles and plain pasta.

GROCERY STORES, GREENGROCERS, AND FARMERS' MARKETS

It's no surprise that fixing your own meals will be your cheapest option. I actually enjoy grocery shopping when I travel because it's a cultural experience and I think looking at the type of foods that are on the shelves is fun.

For the most part, you'll find much of the same food in European grocery stores as you can back home. Space is at a premium in Europe, so expect smaller stores and less variety than what you're accustomed

In a hurry? Stop into a grocery store for pre-made food.

The farmers' market is still a great experience even if you don't buy anything.

to finding. Also be aware that most grocery stores close around 8 p.m. and many are closed or close around noon on Sunday.

Many grocery stores will have prepared sandwiches, wraps, and salads that range from about $5 to $9 if you're looking for something quick and easy. Some shops have special deals where you can get a sandwich or salad with a dessert/fruit and drink for around $8 to $12.

If you're staying at a hostel that has a kitchen, remember that you're still limited in the types of meals you can prepare since you won't have a lot of storage/fridge space for your food. Try to purchase just enough ingredients to make a meal or two.

Another good option is to get a bunch of people together at the hostel and make a big meal. This is a great way to make friends, and the price per person is really low if you get a lot of people to chip in for the meal.

No trip to Europe is complete without a stop at a farmers' market. It is a fun and exciting way to find high-quality food at a good price. Additionally, the quality of food you'll find there will be light-years ahead of the stuff in the grocery store. A money-saving trick is to wait until the market is starting to close because some stalls will discount their goods. You should also shop around because different vendors will have different prices. If there are no markets close to you, another great place to find high-quality fresh produce are at greengrocers. You'll mainly find these shops scattered throughout any city.

STREET FOOD AND BUDGET TAKEOUT RESTAURANTS

Falafels are cheap and taste amazing.

Getting a meal from a street food vendor or budget takeout restaurant is a great way to get a warm, filling meal for a fair price. Each country or region has its own street food specialty—France has crepes, Berlin has currywurst, Belgium has fries with a million types of sauce, pizza slices in Italy, fish and chips in the UK, etc.

The most popular budget meal in Europe would be the Doner Kebab (it's sometimes called shawarma or

Doner kebabs are salty, greasy, and delicious. Plus, they only cost around $6, so it's a great deal for budget travelers.

a gyro). While each country has its own slight variation, a kebab is basically thinly shaved meat (lamb, beef, chicken, or turkey) served in pita bread and topped with lettuce, tomatoes, onions, and a variety of sauces. It's usually served with a side of fries. They are delicious, greasy, very filling, and only cost around $4 to $6. Additionally, shops that sell kebabs also sell other grilled or fried foods that are equally affordable.

And, of course, there are always plenty of cheap Chinese, Thai, Indian, and pizza places in every city. To find the best quality food, you should venture away from the city center and into the immigrant neighborhoods.

Ham, cheese, butter, and bread—it doesn't get any better than that.

145

Another great option for quality affordable food are bakeries. During lunch and dinner, you'll find freshly prepared sandwiches, salads, pizza, quiches, and other items at reasonable prices. For example, in Paris my favorite bakery had a lunch special that included a large baguette sandwich, small dessert, and a soda for about $7.

BUDGET-FRIENDLY RESTAURANTS

You're probably not going to eat many restaurant meals, but when you do, be sure to seek out the best quality for the best price possible. The first step is to follow the locals. The best clue is the menu—if it's written in multiple languages, then you know it is a place for tourists. You'll probably have to venture a few blocks away from the tourist sights before you'll start finding the places where locals eat. It's totally possible to have a quality meal for around $16 (without drinks)

This hearty meal of duck confit only costs around $15.

I rarely use guidebooks to find restaurant recommendations because the information is already a year or two old by the time you're reading it.

That is why I tend to research restaurants online. Sites like TripAdvisor and Yelp are two of the most obvious places to look for reviews. However, I like to tap into the local expat community. Nearly every city will have a few websites written by expats dedicated to finding quality restaurants. Additionally, a quick Google search will bring up hundreds of blog posts and articles about people's favorite restaurants.

OTHER TIPS FOR EATING ON THE CHEAP

Lunch specials. Restaurants across Europe cut their prices during lunch to attract business people on their lunch breaks. Normally, they'll have a set menu with a few different choices that include a starter, main dish, and a dessert. The meals are the same quality as dinner, so this is a great way to have good food without paying a lot.

Share meals and get creative. Street food, like Kebabs for example, are hearty enough to be split between two people. Buy some fruit and a drink from a grocery store and you can easily feed two people for around $6 per person.

Shop at grocery stores. Shopping for food and alcohol at the grocery store will save a lot of money. Most good hostels will have kitchens so you can make your own meals. For lunch, I recommend picking up some basic food for a nice picnic in the park or a public square.

Additionally, buying alcohol at the grocery store and drinking at the hostel or at a park is always a fine option. Most European countries are fairly relaxed about drinking in parks if you don't make a scene.

There are all kinds of great little restaurants, but you just need to know where to look.

Do a little research. As an outsider, it's hard to know exactly where to eat as you travel. Go online and spend an hour writing down a list of cheap restaurants or grocery stores near the areas that you'll be exploring for the day. This way, you'll have a few options of where to eat and you won't waste a lot time trying to find where to go. Trying to do this on the fly via a smartphone is also an option, but I always find it easier to already have options ready.

Eat before you're too hungry. Find a place to eat before you're really hungry. If you wait until you're about to pass out from starvation, you're very likely to eat at the first place you see—which is probably expensive and/or poor quality. This is another reason to carry some snacks with as you travel. Additionally, people tend to get cranky when they're hungry and this just leads to more conflict if you're traveling with other people.

Ask for tap water. If you ask for water at a restaurant, they will nearly always bring you an expensive bottle of water. Tap water is free, but you have to specifically ask for it.

Drinks at the bar. Drink your drink (coffee, tea, beer, wine, hot chocolate, etc.) at the bar and it will usually be cheaper than if you sit at a table.

Drinks are expensive. Visitors are surprised how much soda and bottled water costs in restaurants. And they don't do free refills on soda.

Learn the tipping culture. The tipping customs in Europe are different in each country. However, in general, the tip is already included in your bill. If you want to include a little extra that's fine, but you're probably wasting money if you tip 15%.

Eating outside comes at a premium. Cozying up in a chair on a sidewalk café and people watching is a national sport in Europe, but you'll sometimes pay a little extra for the experience.

Eat the free breakfast. Many hostels include free breakfast—eat it. It is usually bland, but whatever. Go back for seconds if you can.

GET YOUR DRINK ON

Yumm. Beer.

A big night out drinking on the town can quickly bust your budget if you're not careful. The key is finding the best places to go and maybe having a little self-restraint.

Ask hostel workers. The people working at the hostel will usually have their favorite bars, pubs, and cafés so it makes sense to ask them. Ask them where they go after work.

Many hostels organize pub-crawls. However, it would be naive to think that a lot of these hostel workers aren't getting kickbacks from these bars. It may not always be true, but keep in mind that you could find better deals elsewhere.

Grocery stores. It's no surprise that the cheapest alcohol is found at the grocery store. Nearly every store will have a wide selection of wine (especially in regions that make a lot of the stuff) and a variety of beer will also be available. If you want a greater beer selection, you will probably have to go to smaller specialty shops. Also, it is fairly rare to find cold beer in grocery stores, but smaller convenience stores will sell individual bottles that have been chilled.

Student areas. European students enjoying drinking cheaply just as much as you do, so find out where the local students hang out. Almost any major city will have websites dedicated to finding the best drink deals in town—which are often the places that students frequent.

Drink in public. Europe has fairly lax laws (or at least lax enforcement) about drinking in public. This doesn't mean you can walk around the street chugging a beer, but it is often perfectly acceptable to enjoy a beer or a bottle of wine in a park or other spaces. The police won't bother you if you're respectable and don't make a scene.

Grab some beer and wine. Head down to the river and enjoy. It's perfectly legal!

Discount Cards, Museum Passes, and Student Discounts

The **International Student Identity Card** (ISIC) is the only internationally recognized student ID for full-time students and it costs $25. The card gives you thousands of discounts all across Europe on things like tours, restaurants, shops, and other attractions. It also includes some basic travel insurance for your trip. However, 99% of the discounts are to places you'd probably never go in the first place. There are a few decent discounts like no booking fees at Hostelworld.com that will save you $2 per booking. Some hostels might give you 5% to 10% off.

Visit Isic.org to see which discounts you can get based on where you're going to visit.

The main benefit of the card is to prove to museums that you're a student and that usually means you'll get free or reduced entry. Many students have used their **student IDs** from back home with success, but I have been turned away from using my student ID because it didn't have a date on it. The card is only $25 so even if it gets you into two museums for free, it has already paid for itself.

London, Paris, Berlin, Amsterdam, and most other major cities sell some sort of **tourist card** that gives you unlimited access to museums, monuments, and public transportation. These cards lure you in with the prospect of free entry into dozens of museums and they tell you that you'll save hundreds of dollars. In reality, the cards may not be such a hot deal—it all depends on your travel style.

The problem with these cards is that you typically need to visit a lot of attractions to get your value out of the card. Sometimes you need to visit two or three museums/attractions a day to break even. Personally, I can only spend so much time at a museum before I start going crazy. You will have to do a little strategic logistical planning to ensure you maximize the card's value.

The best thing about the pass is the ability to skip the ticket lines. During the busy season, this can easily save you an hour or more each day. However, more and more attractions are starting to sell e-tickets on their websites, so check out that option. For some travelers, these tourist cards can be an excellent deal, but I urge you to examine it closely because you might end up wasting a lot of money.

Use Public Transportation

Whether it's the bus, tram, or subway, you're going to want to take public transportation during your trip because it's fast, efficient, and affordable. Most cities offer multiple passes so it's wise to study the different options. A majority of visitors automatically opt for an unlimited day pass or a multi-day pass. These can be a good deal if you plan on using it multiple times a day. At the very least, compare the price of day passes to the price of a single ticket so you can see how many rides are needed to break even. However, a day pass does give you the convenience of only needing to buy one ticket and you won't feel guilty for taking short jaunts.

Normally, you can purchase tickets from ticket machines or at the ticket window inside the station. On buses and some trams, you can purchase a ticket from the drivers. Each city has its own system so you'll need to do a little research. Ticket machines will take coins and/ or cash. Some will take credit cards but American cards may not work so it's a good idea to have coins.

In many cities, public transportation has no ticket takers so you're kind of on the honor system. I saw multiple people jump the turnstiles every day on the Paris Metro. You may even find yourself wanting to do the same thing, but the fines can be steep if you get caught. I jumped the turnstile once in Paris because the machine wouldn't take my ticket and, about fifteen minutes later, ticket inspectors came around checking tickets. I tried to plead my innocence, but they weren't interested in my story. I was fined about $45 and I had to pay right then. In other cities, it is common for plain-clothes officers to randomly check tickets.

London's Oyster Card makes using the Underground a breeze.

Additionally, don't forget to **validate your ticket**. On most subways, you insert the ticket into the turnstiles at the entrance of the station and that validates the ticket. But some cities don't have turnstiles, so you simply walk into the station and find the machine that validates the ticket. On trams and buses, the validation boxes are inside by the doors. Riding with a non-validated ticket is the same as riding without a ticket so don't forget.

Random Helpful Tips

Here is a list of random tips that I've discovered during my travels. Most don't have anything to do with money, but they're things you can do to have a more enjoyable adventure.

Don't feel bad about being a tourist. A lot of "elitist" travelers shun anything that is remotely touristy. But just because something is touristy doesn't make it bad. It'd be a shame to skip the Eiffel Tower just because it's one of the biggest tourist attractions in the world. What you actually want to do is avoid tourist traps. Of course you should seek out the local culture; don't get so caught up in the idea that you must act like a "local" all the time to have an "authentic" experience.

Prepare for burnout. Not many people talk about it, but most travelers reach a certain point in their trip where they start to feel burned out. This is especially true for people that travel at a breakneck pace, but nearly everyone will feel it at some point. For most people, it kicks in around week two or three. It's perfectly normal, so don't worry. Take some time to do normal stuff. Go see a movie. Spend a few hours relaxing with a book in a park. Just walk around.

Sometimes you need to get away from the hustle and bustle. Remember to take time to chill out.

A lot of people resist doing these "normal" things because they feel like they're wasting their trip but it's not true. You need time to recharge your batteries, and the more you put it off, the more it will affect your travels.

Learn about the city and get a little exercise.

151

Take a walking or bike tour. Every city in Europe is filled with amazing stories and they're drenched in history, but most visitors just wander around and have no idea what they're looking at. A walking tour or a bike tour will give your visit some historical context that greatly adds to your experience.

New Europe Tours (neweuropetours.com) offers free walking tours of many major cities across Europe. The guides are normally students or young people, but they do work for tips so it isn't totally free. I've been on a few and they're usually pretty good. The groups can get pretty big since they're free/cheap. New Europe isn't the only free tour company so you should be able to find many options.

Just about any city will have companies that have paid tours that are run by qualified tour guides. Many tours will revolve around a theme (food, neighborhoods, time period, ghost/haunted, culture, etc.), so you can find something tailored to your interests. Walking tours usually cost anywhere from $15 to $20 and bike tours normally cost $20 to $40.

Finally, if you're really on a tight budget, there are plenty of self-guided walking tours found in guidebooks. Most bookstores will also have a handful of books dedicated to self-guided walking tours. If you hate reading, you can also download audio city guides.

Seek out special experiences. Do something active every once in a while. Take a cooking class. Go to a sporting event. Go skydiving. Go biking. Rent a scooter for the day. These experiences will be the things you remember most from your trip.

Paragliding over the Swiss Alps is one of my favorite memories. It wasn't cheap, but it's an adventure I'll never forget.

Plan your day. Before you head off for a day of sightseeing, spend some time planning out your day. Don't create a minute-by-minute itinerary but jot down a list of things you might want to see or do. The idea is to create a little structure while still allowing plenty of freedom. If there are specific things you want to see, it's smart to know if they're closed on a certain day of the week.

If there is a certain museum or attraction you want to see, you should go online to see if you can purchase tickets from their website or if tickets are sold elsewhere. You might be able to save yourself from having to wait in line for an hour.

Keep a journal. Spend a little time each day writing about the things you've done. Write about what you ate or if you had an encounter with a crazy person. Write down train times and addresses. By the end of your trip, it will be an awesome souvenir.

Relax. Stuff is going to go wrong. You'll mess up. You'll fight with your travel partner. You need to learn how to roll with the punches or you will go crazy. If you feel yourself starting to get stressed, take a step back and remember that this is all part of the experience.

Get offline. Being connected to the Internet is great and it can make traveling easier. But it's also easy to focus so much on posting photos online and communicating to people back home that you take yourself out of the moment. You end up disconnecting from what you've traveled across the world to see.

Many cities have public bike-sharing programs. In Paris, there are 14,000 bicycles and 1,230 bicycle stations throughout the city.

Take photos of yourself. I have thousands of photos from my travels but I only have a few with me in them. Not taking more photos with me (and my travel partners) in them is one of the things I regret the most. Don't be afraid to ask strangers to take your photos because most of the time they want someone to take their photo, as well.

Wander. Don't be afraid to simply wander aimlessly around cities. Get lost. Maybe you'll find some cool things to see. If nothing else, you'll get to glimpse peoples' everyday lives.

Travel cities by bike. One of the best ways to explore a city is by bike. It's relaxing and you can cover a huge amount of ground. Many cities have free/cheap bike rental programs that let anyone rent a bike for short periods of time. Additionally, any city will have companies that rent bikes.

Learn some of the language. No one expects you to learn the local languages, but knowing just a few small words can be a huge help. Write down the basics like "yes," "no," "please," and "thank you." Most travel books have a language section or you can purchase a small language phrasebook.

Value versus price. Traveling on a budget isn't always about doing things as cheaply as possible. It's also about getting the maximum amount of value for your money. Sometimes spending a little extra will result in a large jump in value, so take that into consideration. For example, paying a few extra dollars on a hostel located in an amazing location might be worth it because your overall enjoyment will be much higher than staying at the cheap hostel on the edge of town.

Take it all in. Cherish the moment and stop thinking about what to do or see next. Soak in the atmosphere and realize how fortunate you are to have such a great experience. Appreciate this time while it lasts.

ACKNOWLEDGMENTS

I'd like to take a moment to thank everyone who helped me write this book. First of all, I wanted to thank my wife, Susan, not only for listening to me ramble about this book over the past few months, but for also being my travel partner. I can't wait to see where our next adventure takes us. I also want to thank my parents because they both worked hard to ensure we always went on family vacations every summer. And, without their support, I wouldn't have been able to travel abroad in the first place.

INDEX